IT'S TIME
TO TALK
ABOUT RACE
AT WORK

IT'S TIME
TO TALK
ABOUT RACE
AT WORK

EVERY LEADER'S GUIDE TO MAKING PROGRESS ON DIVERSITY, EQUITY, AND INCLUSION

KELLY McDONALD

WILEY

Published by John Wiley & Sons, Inc., Hoboken, New Jersey.
Published simultaneously in Canada.

For general information on our other products and services or for technical support, please contact our Customer Care Department within the United States at (800) 762-2974, outside the United States at (317) 572-3993 or fax (317) 572-4002.

Wiley publishes in a variety of print and electronic formats and by print-on-demand. Some material included with standard print versions of this book may not be included in e-books or in print-on-demand. If this book refers to media such as a CD or DVD that is not included in the version you purchased, you may download this material at http://booksupport.wiley.com. For more information about Wiley products, visit www.wiley.com.

Library of Congress Cataloging-in-Publication Data:

Names: McDonald, Kelly, 1961- author. | John Wiley & Sons, publisher.
Title: It's time to talk about race at work : every leader's guide to
   making progress on diversity, equity, and inclusion / Kelly McDonald.
Description: Hoboken, New Jersey : Wiley, [2021] | Includes index.
Identifiers: LCCN 2021008528 (print) | LCCN 2021008529 (ebook) | ISBN
   9781119790877 (cloth) | ISBN 9781119790884 (adobe pdf) | ISBN
   9781119790891 (epub)
Subjects: LCSH: Diversity in the workplace.
Classification: LCC HF5549.5.M5 M426 2021 (print) | LCC HF5549.5.M5
   (ebook) | DDC 658.3008–dc23
LC record available at https://lccn.loc.gov/2021008528
LC ebook record available at https://lccn.loc.gov/2021008529

Cover image: Getty Images | W RPHT WPHAKDI PHECHR / EYEEM
Cover design: Paul McCarthy

Printed in the United States of America

SKY10025969_042921

To Liliana Ramírez, for all the brilliant insights from your brilliant mind.
To JB, for hanging in there with me on this. Again.
And to George.

Do the best you can until you know better.
Then when you know better, do better.
—Maya Angelou

Contents

Acknowledgments   xvii

Special Acknowledgments   xxi

PART I   If You're Not Racist, What's the Problem? The Biggest Mistakes People (and Businesses) Make   1

Chapter 1   This Book Is for Everyone, but Especially White Readers   3
- Most White people would rather *not* talk about race
- Who this book is for (I'm betting you fall into one of these categories)
- What this book is—and *isn't* (*Hint:* It's not a book about activism or social injustice)

Chapter 2 **You're Not Racist, but You Have Blind Spots** 13
- Bias can lead to blind spots
- Don't be defensive: we all have bias—even babies have bias
- The weird things we do to justify our business decisions

Chapter 3 **The High Cost of Bias: Why All-White or Mostly White Businesses Make Less Money** 21
- How one of the biggest (and almost all-White) industries lost customers and revenue—and how they fixed the problem
- Signs that your business may be missing out on opportunities

Chapter 4 **The Business Case for Diversity** 29
- Discover diversity's "secret sauce"—the one monumental ingredient that makes diversity rock
- And what happens when that ingredient is missing

Chapter 5 **The Excuses People Use to Avoid Doing Anything about Diversity** 37
- "We can't find any qualified diverse candidates"
- "We hire for quality, not for color"
- "It would be unfair to a more qualified candidate"
- "We already know a very good candidate in our network"
- "We hired/promoted a diverse person once and they failed"
- "Our customers won't be comfortable with a diverse person"
- "Our competitors aren't diverse either, so it's not a problem"
- "We looked into diversity—it's too expensive to implement"

Chapter 6   **Well-Intentioned Things White People Say That Are Hurtful or Offensive to Others   45**
- "I don't see color/I don't care what color you are"
- "I treat everyone the same"
- "I'm not racist or biased"
- Three better ways to express that you value diversity and aren't racist

Chapter 7   **Why Your Diversity, Equity, and Inclusion Efforts Haven't Done the Job   51**
- Five big reasons
- At work, the subject of racism has been taboo
- Specific ways to start conversations about race with colleagues
  o In one-on-one conversations
  o In a meeting
- Corporate America gets real and acknowledges failures
- Why we have to stop singing "We Are the World"—and be brave enough to use the word *racism*

PART II   **How to Talk about Race at Work   63**

Chapter 8   **How to Talk about Race in Helpful and Positive Ways: Do's and Don'ts   65**
- EEK! Why is this so hard?
- Sincerity matters
- Don't apologize for being White, but acknowledge that people of color are often treated differently than Whites in our society
- Start small: six ways to start the conversation on the right foot
- What to say, what *NOT* to say—and *why*
- How to handle friction or conflict in constructive ways
- How to recover when you've blown it unintentionally

Chapter 9   **Answers to Tough Employee Questions and Racist Remarks   77**
- "Shouldn't we just hire the most qualified person?"
- "All this talk about race—we're all one race, the human race!"
- "I came from nothing and pulled myself up by my bootstraps. No one helped me. Why do we need to do something special for minorities?"
- What to do if an employee makes a racist statement online

Chapter 10   **Where to Start When You Don't Know Where to Start: Eight Steps to Making Progress on DE&I   87**
- Everything you feel comfortable doing is something you had to *learn*—you can learn how to do this, too
- The STARTING Method: Sincerity, Transparency, Acknowledgment, Respect, Tools, Investment, Nurturing Talent, Goals

PART III   **Making Diversity, Equity, and Inclusion Real   107**

Chapter 11   **How to Build Business Relationships with People Different Than You   109**
- A brewery serves "diversity on tap"—and makes its mark in a non-diverse community
- What if I don't know any people of color?
- Truth breeds trust—be upfront and honest about your diversity issues and goals
- Show up and help first before you ask for help
- Personal contact, interaction, and conversations bring about more behavior and attitude change than training

Chapter 12   **What to Do If You See or Hear Casual Racism or Sexism at Work   117**
- Doing nothing creates one of two kinds of guilt
  - Personal guilt
  - Collective guilt—this one is worse
- The bystander effect
- Five effective tactics to use, whether you're the target or a bystander

Chapter 13   Recruiting and Interviewing Diverse Candidates   127
  - Eliminate inherent bias
    o Stop "picturing" your ideal candidate
    o Rewrite your job descriptions to remove bias
  - Do's and don'ts for writing more inclusive job descriptions
  - How to find diverse talent—six effective no-cost/ low-cost tactics
  - How to interview diverse candidates—six best practices

Chapter 14   Mentoring, Networking, and Checking In: Three Big Ways You Can Help Your Diverse Employees Succeed   137
  - It's not coddling—it's your job
  - Their success is your success
  - Your support is not favoritism: four reasons why it's fair
  - Your advocacy can be a game-changer

PART IV   Lead Your Colleagues, Customers, Partners, and Employees   147

Chapter 15   The Leader's Role: Guiding and Setting the Example   149
  - If you are a White male in a leadership role, you can have a greater impact than anyone
    o Your views on diversity are seen as "neutral" and credible (not so for women and minorities)
    o Here's your chance to make a real difference
  - Lead by example—walk the talk
    o It starts with naming the elephant in the room—if you can't do it, who can?
    o Foster safe discussion of touchy issues by modeling how to address them head-on
    o What to say and do when horrific and racist things happen in the world—eight do's and don'ts

Chapter 16   Reducing Tokenism and Bias: Give Your Diverse Employees and Suppliers a Genuine Seat at the Table   159
- Five do's and don'ts for avoiding tokenism in hiring
- Two key steps to avoid tokenism in professional development and promotions

Chapter 17   Dealing with Naysayers and Derailers   167
- Three ways to deal with naysayers
- The different types of derailers and their motivations
- You can change the people—or "change the people"

Chapter 18   You're Not Finished. Keep Trying. Keep Evolving.   175
- Worst thing you can do: "launch and abandon"
- Do's & don'ts for maintaining traction
  - Assess progress/address problems
  - Don't be afraid to refine it along the way
  - Expect to educate/and repeat/and repeat
  - Keep your ear to the ground/listen to the hallway chatter
  - Celebrate success
  - Set new goals and strategies to strengthen ongoing efforts

Appendix   Helpful Terms and Resources   181
Helpful Terms
- BIPOC
- DE&I
- Definitions of Diversity, Equity, and Inclusion
- LGBTQ+
- POC
- Structural Racism
- Systemic Racism
- White Privilege

Helpful Resources
- Best Job Boards for Diversity and Inclusion
- Energetic Awakenings
- *Harvard Business Review*'s 10 Must-Reads on Diversity
- LinkedIn's Diversity Recruiting Guide

Index   187

Acknowledgments

I started writing this book in September 2020 and finished it in early January 2021. It was a dark time to take on this subject: Life and business were disrupted immeasurably due to the COVID-19 pandemic. Nationwide unrest, protests, riots, and violence seemed a part of daily life.

I am an optimist at heart—not in a rainbows and unicorns unrealistic way, but I do believe in hope. As the grind of the pandemic and faltering economy wore on, I found my nerves frayed and saw the same in others. I needed an anchor, a way of staying focused on knowing what I can control and what I can't, and a way of remaining hopeful when hope seemed like more of a concept than an actual feeling. I decided to anchor myself to the word *resilience*. Every day, I see resilient people, moving forward against difficult odds, facing their fears and obstacles, overcoming setbacks, and extending generosity to others. It's easy to be generous when times are good. What is deeply moving to me is seeing generosity when times are challenging.

Everyone had their own struggles, their own problems, and their own burdens in 2020, yet so many people helped me with this book. I needed their help.

I am a White woman, and I was writing a book about race and how to talk about it at work. I don't have the personal experiences and insights that people of color and other minority groups have. I needed different perspectives to illustrate a complete picture of the challenges of talking about race at work. In the beginning of this book project, I told a few people in my circle what I was doing and why. Their responses were immediate, generous, and, for some, very time intensive. From "I know someone you should talk to" or "I have an example you might be able to use" to simply "What can I do to help?" their eagerness to assist and their contributions blew me away. They contributed stories, insights, and experiences because they believe what I believe: *We grow stronger when we confront our problems rather than ignore them.* If we talk about our problems, we can solve them or, at a minimum, make inroads on solutions. And when we work with people who are not like us, we become smarter—and better. I believe this with all my heart, and I am inspired that so many others feel the same.

There is no way I will ever be able to fully express my gratitude to all those in my life and in my orbit who helped in ways big and small, but I'll try my best:

To Richard Narramore, my editor, for keenly understanding what business book readers need—and why. For fostering the conversations that most people don't want to have and don't know how to approach. I'm thankful for your steady hand on the rudder when I veered off course. And for all the hours on the phone with me and the countless emails on New Year's Eve day to help me finish the manuscript on time. I say this with every new book, but I mean it more each time: I am grateful that out of all the editors in the world, you're mine.

To Deborah Schindlar, Victoria Anllo, Angela Morrison, and the entire team at Wiley, for developing and creating great books that help move business forward. Thank you for supporting me and sharing my conviction that diversity is a powerful business tool.

To Pam Atherton, for sending relevant content and contacts my way before I ever even asked. For the texts and calls and gifs and memes that kept me going. For your thoughtful commentary on subjects important—and mundane. Sometimes, the mundane ones are the best ones.

To Cliff Bohaker, for always making the effort to stay in touch with calls, videos, texts, and visits. I am not sure which of those are the most ridiculous—keep 'em coming! I love you and our adventures.

To Carrie Bratcher: You and I were emailing about work stuff when I got the call with the approval for this book. You were the first person I told about it, and thirty minutes later, you sent me content that you thought might be helpful. Yep. You're amazing.

To Jess and Rich Fierro, for taking the time to share their vision and story with me. You truly "walk the talk" and set an inspiring example of how business is better when diversity is on tap.

To Tamara Ghandour, for being the break I needed, whenever I needed it. Thank you for the laughs, the insights, the never-ending fun, the juicy stories about *everything* under the sun, the shared Reese's, Bang drinks, and peanut crack. You're wicked smart and wicked funny and you charge my battery every time we get together.

To Chris Heim at AbeTech, for being terrific to work with and an inspiration every day. I love the way your mind works and your devotion to servant leadership. The world needs more people like you.

To Quiana Hughes, for your time, your insights, your stories, and your experiences. Your input helped shape this book and got me out of the gate. I'm game for dinner again *anytime*—I adore you.

To Kiki: You made sheltering at home in 2020 bearable. Thanks for watching trashy TV with me in the evenings when I needed to unwind.

To Jenny Krummenacher and the entire diversity team at Zebra Technologies, for "walking the walk" on diversity, equity, and inclusion and allowing me to be a Zebra too. And to Nena Petrunic Brichetto, Galy Navarro, Caroline Zepeda, Helle Terp Kidbane, and Julia Roberts: You are the BEST. And so, so fun.

To Jennifer Martin, the first to call me when my mom passed away. I'll never forget your voicemail message of simply, "Kelly, I got you." Thank you for always being there for me, no matter how much time has passed between our talks. And to Joe Martin and Jake Martin, my "other family members": I love you.

To my siblings, Randi and Mike, for the meaningful reconnection and support and gift of real family.

To Randy Pierce, my friend and my coach, for teaching me so much more than boxing. I cherish our conversations, your insights, and your humor. You have the ability to make me laugh harder than I thought I could, and you've changed my life in more ways than you'll *ever* know.

To Kenja Purkey, for getting this topic and getting me in general. For taking my calls *whenever*. For never, ever losing your sense of humor, even when you're juggling more than anyone else I know. #RighteousKenja

To Bill Sandberg: You're a great boxing partner and friend and I'll spar with you anytime. Glove up and I'll see you in the ring!

To Sally Shoquist, for the laughs and rants—and then more laughs. I feel better after every call with you and after every one of your amazing salads. Looking forward to sitting on your deck with you on more sunny afternoons.

To Robert Swafford: Without you, I wouldn't have the circle of friends I have. Thanks for always being there for me and for being the head of the octopus in our group.

To Lynne Swihart: Your friendship, snark, and wit are the gas in my tank. Here's to the next decade of our close friendship and escapades.

To my clients, who became my friends. You have cheered me on, encouraged me and you're the reason I do what I do. Special shout-outs to Joe Aldez, Ron Arrigo, Steven Braybrook, Susan Freibrun and the entire staff of MHEDA, Erika Goode, Cris Hay-Merchant, Jeff Hurt, Bill Lewis, Lynne Marchese, Kathleen Overlin, Liz Richards, Vince Rodriguez, Chuck Rusch, Bill Rutherford, Team Zebra, Brett Vanderkolk, Liz Walz, Lola Woloch, and Terry Young.

And to every reader of this book: You know why this topic matters and why it matters now. I may never know you, but I know your intentions. You make a difference. *Thank you.*

Special Acknowledgments

When I started writing this book, I needed perspective, expertise, and insights from people who are professionally immersed in diversity, equity, and inclusion. DE&I is a critically important topic—and a sensitive one. I needed expert help to create a realistic path of progress that anyone, at any size organization, could follow. Not every business has a Diversity Department or even an HR professional. Small business owners need realistic and actionable tactics that don't cost a million dollars or take a year to get off the ground. I needed the help of people who understood exactly what readers of this book want and need, and I reached out to Liliana Ramírez, Joy Pierce, and David Phillips.

Many, many people contributed to making this book come to life, but these experts shared their wisdom, experiences, approaches, findings, and advice, freely and generously. Each heads up a business or department, so they have their own demanding, full-time roles, yet they made time for this book. Their commitment and dedication to this book cannot be overstated. I am deeply grateful to them and wish to acknowledge their significant contributions:

To Liliana Ramírez, for your tireless efforts, over *months*, and your commitment to helping businesspeople develop effective and realistic diversity programs. For nearly two decades, I've been in awe of your work, your humor, your patience, the way your mind works, and your ability to always see the path forward, no matter how complicated or unclear. Without your research, this book would not exist. Without your insights, our readers would not have a usable framework for talking about race at work. Your time, dedication, and focus ensured we met every deadline, took care of every client and every project, and created a book we both believe in. I'll never be able to fully express my gratitude.

To Joy Pierce, for your vast and important contributions to this book. Your examples, suggested approaches, candor, insights, and complete willingness to help me when you didn't even know me speaks to your generous heart and desire to create change. Our first phone call lasted *three hours* and we both know it could have gone on forever. You took every call from me, regardless of whether it was day or night, and responded to every text and query to keep me moving and on track to meet my deadlines. You started off as a valued resource, but you became my friend. You're stuck with me now.

To David Phillips, for your insights, anecdotes, experience, proven techniques, and recommendations on how to talk about difficult topics in productive and constructive ways. You made this book a priority and your contributions are matched only by your passion and commitment to a better world for everyone.

Liliana Ramírez
President, LunaNova
Marketing—Diversity and
Communications
Strategy for the World

Joy Pierce, Ph.D.
Associate Professor,
University of Utah

David deBardelaben-
Phillips
Founder and President
Energetic Awakenings

IT'S TIME
TO TALK
ABOUT RACE
AT WORK

PART I

If You're Not Racist, What's the Problem? The Biggest Mistakes People (and Businesses) Make

CHAPTER 1
This Book Is for Everyone, but Especially White Readers

The topic of race and diversity at work is a BIG DEAL—every aspect of it: building a more diverse team, making your business more inclusive, recruiting diverse new talent, rethinking business practices to make them more equitable, and more. And yet it's hard to talk about. Much of the language of diversity and the very concepts that create problems around diversity, such as systemic racism and White privilege, seem to have been adopted by the progressive left and that's a turn-off to people on the right.

As you read this book, you may disagree with many phrases and concepts. You may have "diversity fatigue." You may roll your eyes at the concept of inequity. Even if you disagree with the language or concepts, I know you'll be on board with how diversity can help grow your business: better employee talent, greater levels of retention and engagement, more innovation, better customer experiences, higher satisfaction levels, and greater sales and profits—that's language that *everyone* likes.

But here's some real talk: Most White people would rather *not* go there. They'd rather not talk about race and diversity because it's scary, exhausting, overwhelming, and "a pain to deal with." It's easy to say the wrong thing and face criticism. And at some organizations, diversity training feels more like "shame and blame" than skills building. Of course, the situation for many people of color is worse—they are missing out on opportunities for networking, jobs, promotions, and income because Whites are reluctant to talk about and address race and diversity issues.

On top of that, diversity has now become a major political hot potato. Much of the world is deeply divided on the issue of race, and it is extremely difficult to say *anything* without alienating half the population. We've lost our way when it comes to having sensible, constructive conversations about race. That's exactly what I am trying to do in this book: provide realistic, doable, productive tools and insights that will help you have the conversations you may not really want to have—or that you have no idea *how* to have. It's about *skills*, not holding hands and singing "Kumbaya."

If you're on the left, you might criticize this book for not taking more of an activist view and for speaking and writing as bluntly as I do. If you're on the right, you might criticize this book because you believe that systemic racism is overblown, that it is just a new trendy buzzword phrase and one more example of political correctness run amok. Whichever way you lean, whatever you believe, this book will show you how to talk about race and diversity at work.

I'm White. I started writing this book primarily with White readers in mind, because White businesspeople tend to assume a White perspective on things. We don't know what it's like to be "the only" in the room: the only Black person, the only Asian person, the only Hispanic person, or the only Middle Eastern person, for example. We don't know what it's like to worry about being considered for a promotion, and then if we get it, worrying about whether we are the token of diversity and that our company can now "check that off the list." We don't know what it's like to have someone at work tell us we should go by another name so that we blend in better. (Yes, this happens. My friend Leroy is a tall, dark-skinned Black man. He sells high-end luxury cars and has a strong track record of sales. His coworker suggested he would "do better and seem less threatening" if he changed his name to Doug at work.)

White people in leadership can be oblivious. It's not intentional. It's simply the lens through which we view the world. We can't *consider* different perspectives if we don't *hear* different perspectives. And we can't hear them if we surround ourselves with people who are just like us.

My perspective on diversity, equity, and inclusion comes from more than two decades of work on this subject. I'm a professional speaker and have written three bestselling books on diversity, all from *the standpoint of business*. I work with all kinds of companies and all kinds of people: large Fortune 500 companies and small business owners, diversity champions and diversity skeptics. The response to my books and presentations is always positive, especially among White people, because Whites simply do not know how to talk about race and diversity. When we don't know what to do, we do nothing, and that's not good for business growth and success. Another reason that the response to my perspective on diversity has always been positive is that I don't try to change how people feel about diversity. People have very complex emotions surrounding this topic, from fear to guilt to resentment to helplessness and more. I start with one basic truth that everyone agrees with: *Business is not about dealing with the world the way you want the world to be. It's about dealing with the world the way the world is.* Framed in this way, the topic of diversity is more palatable to most people. I'm not trying to change hearts and minds. I'm trying to change *business*.

Make no mistake: I believe that only good things come from a more diverse workplace, and I cover all of those in Chapter 4. And I believe that we benefit as a society and as people if we make progress on diversity, equity, and inclusion. But this book is focused on the skills you need to talk about a key issue that affects *business*.

You're focused on this issue, too. You're on the first chapter of a book that will show you how you can help—*actually, truly, measurably, and meaningfully help*. You're a businessperson. The way that you can help is through your company, team, and customers. You can help create a fair, equitable, and inclusive workplace for everyone, and by doing that, you can literally help change the world.

Right now, you could be doing any number of fun things: playing with your kids, talking with a friend, making a meal, watching your favorite TV show, working out, researching your next vacation, eating ice cream! But you're not. You're reading a book on how to talk about race and diversity at work and hoping you'll get some insights and tips for making your workplace or teams *better*. Better for *all*. You are investing your time *right now* in learning how to talk about and address a topic that is important and *uncomfortable*.

HOW DID WE GET HERE?

For a while, it felt as if we were lulled into thinking we, as a society, had made some progress! After all, the U.S. had a Black president for eight years, so how bad could racism still be?

On May 25, 2020, we found out exactly how bad it could be. On that date, George Floyd died on a street in Minneapolis, pinned to the ground, as four police officers sat on him and one knelt on his carotid artery. It took eight minutes and forty-six seconds for George Floyd to die. Later, we learned this was actually even longer than we thought: Nine minutes and twenty-nine seconds. *And we watched it happen.*

Suddenly, the problem of racism was no longer abstract. The terrible, awful, chilling, stomach-turning death of George Floyd made us—*and especially White people*—realize that, despite whatever progress we think we've made, the world is *not* equal for everyone. Many of us responded the only way we knew how: by saying, "Enough is enough" and "Things MUST change."

It was an historic moment. Millions of people took to the streets to march for racial equality. Thousands of companies and businesses took a hard look at their own organizations and asked, "How can we do better?" It didn't just happen in the United States; millions of people in all parts of the *world* marched for weeks, demanding justice and change. It happened in cities. It happened in small, rural towns where almost everyone is White. Old and young, of every color, every race, *everywhere*, said, "We have to do something. *Now*." But what? What do we do?

THIS BOOK IS A STARTING POINT TO A MORE INCLUSIVE WORKPLACE

It's OK to be uncertain about what to do. You want to make a difference, but at some companies, the emphasis on diversity, equity, and inclusion has been heavy-handed. It feels like "marching orders" instead of being part of positive change. Perhaps you feel skeptical or mistrustful about diversity efforts, like you're standing on shifting ground, because at any moment, you could say the wrong thing and someone will yell, "Gotcha!". If you're White, you may feel like *anything* you do may be "wrong," misinterpreted, or misunderstood and backfire or blow up in your face. You may be nervous and conflicted because you genuinely and sincerely want to help and make a difference, but you don't know the way forward. And you're uncomfortable.

Whether you're White, Black, Indigenous, or a person of color, male or female, non-binary or trans, gay or straight, old or young, left-leaning or right-leaning, a leader or business owner or employee, this book can be helpful to you. You will learn what to do—and what not to do—to have constructive conversations about race, not from an activism standpoint, but from a *business* standpoint. In Chapter 10, you'll learn the STARTING Method, an eight-step framework that will show you, step-by-step, how to become a more diverse and inclusive company, department, or team.

But to begin our journey, let's start with who you, the reader, are and what this book is—and isn't.

Who This Book Is For

Readers who will benefit the most from reading this book will fall into a few specific categories:

- The CEO, president, business owner, or business leader who recognizes that their company or enterprise is not very diverse and that this is a real business problem that negatively affects the organization's performance, growth, and profit.
- The executive who has been tasked by their organization to lead, create, expand, or improve their DE&I (diversity, equity, and inclusion) efforts internally.
- The team leader who does not have a diverse team and wants to change that in a relevant way, bringing new talent, skills, and perspective that avoids tokenism.
- The team leader who does have a diverse team, but recognizes that some members of the team may not feel included or heard or perhaps have not received the same chances and opportunities for professional development and advancement as others have.
- The coworker or colleague who is struggling to work alongside people who are different and is afraid to say anything that may not be "politically correct" because they fear being fired or labeled as racist, sexist, homophobic, xenophobic, etc.
- The coworker or colleague who is culturally aware and sensitive to the inequity of others ("woke") and wants to be an effective ally to diverse team members.
- The person who wants to be a better neighbor, friend, volunteer, community member, parent, teacher, partner, client, customer, civil servant, business owner, or church member—in other words, anyone who just wants to be a better *person*.

What This Book Is—and Isn't

Let me tell you what this book is *not*. This is not a book about activism. It is not a book about racial or social injustice. While the very topic of diversity must encompass the *recognition* that our society, and especially the workplace, is not currently racially or socially just, this book will not be dissecting root causes, nor will it be lamenting the impact and effect of such injustice.

This is a business book. This book will show you, as a businessperson, why identifying and addressing your diversity blind spots is important to your business. It is a practical road map from a business perspective, not a bunch of theory, to help you get started.

I will take you through the problems that most businesses have with diversity efforts, the most common mistakes that businesses make when trying to create a diverse and inclusive work culture, and the obstacles that can derail diversity initiatives and give diversity a bad name.

This book is titled *It's Time to Talk about Race at Work*, but shouldn't we have been talking about it before? Yes. *Absolutely.* As a society, we should have talked about race a long time ago, and this conversation is long overdue. For businesses, it's been a challenge, because while many, many companies and organizations have created diversity initiatives, programs, recruiting methods, and training, they haven't done a good job with how to *really talk about race at work,* how to identify and work through the obstacles, discomfort, and tension to build effective plans that tackle these thorny subjects. Our inability to talk about race was the catalyst for this book, but I believe that it's hard for us to talk about diversity and our differences in general. Throughout this book, I will use examples of different kinds of diversity that we encounter at work. Race is the anchor, but women, people of color, LGBTQ+, those who have disabilities, those of different generations and religious groups, and more will also be discussed.

In writing this book, I found myself often overwhelmed with the sheer complexity of it. There are a million facets and layers and I struggled with what to cover and what to leave out. I could fill five books on this topic and never cover it all. This book is designed to get you *started*—to help you have the conversations you need to have but are anxious about having. You'll become more comfortable with what is currently uncomfortable. It will provide you skills that can get us all talking to each other and maybe, just *maybe*, help in narrowing the huge divide we all feel.

You picked up this book for a reason. You're a good person—and you're also brave. It takes bravery to talk about subjects that make people squirm. It takes courage to say, "We can do better. We can be better." It takes commitment to start somewhere. So let's get started.

CHAPTER 2
You're Not Racist, but You Have Blind Spots

Did you know that babies have bias? Several studies show that babies as young as *three months* exhibit bias. Researchers have found that six- to eight-month-old infants are more inclined to learn information from an adult of his or her own race than from an adult of a different race. Babies of any age gaze longer and are more likely to follow visual cues of people of the same race. And babies associate positive music with people of the same race and sad music with people of different races.

How is this possible? How can *babies* be prejudiced? Where and how do they learn something so destructive at such a young age? The answer is that they don't learn it. And they're not prejudiced. They're *biased*.

Bias does not mean *prejudice*. *Bias* means *preference*. The *Collins English Dictionary* definition of *bias* is this: "Bias is a tendency to prefer one person or thing to another, and to favor that person or thing." Babies who are just 90 days old cannot possibly be prejudiced, but they can show preference toward own-race faces over other-race faces. When it comes to learning (which is pretty much all that babies do, besides eating and sleeping), studies show that infants are more inclined to learn information from an adult of his or her own race than from an adult of a different race, especially when it comes to learning under uncertainty.

This observation is important to know and understand because it means that bias is in us. We are born with it. All of us. It does not mean we are born prejudiced; it just means that we have an innate, inherent preference for people who are like us. This probably isn't that shocking when you think about how the human species has survived all these years. We gravitated to, and stayed with, tribes and communities of people who looked like us because that meant safety and protection. Our very survival depended on it. With babies, their first visual contact of other people is usually their parents who are of the same race as they are, and because they form a preference for their parents (and what they look like), they feel safety, trust, or protection when looking at someone who looks like they do.

One of the things I found most fascinating about the various "babies and bias" studies is that babies are not negatively biased toward other races; they are simply *positively biased toward their own race*. In other words, they show *preference* for their own-race faces. That's exactly what bias is—preference, not necessarily prejudice.

No one wants to think of themselves as biased, but if you're going to make progress on race and diversity at work, you have to realize that most people, probably including you, have racial preferences, or unconscious bias. Your natural reaction to this may understandably be an immediate, emphatic, and indignant rebuttal: "I'm not biased! I am the least prejudiced person in this company! My brother is gay, and my sister's husband is Black, and my best friend is from another country!!!" and so on. Why do people have such a strong reaction to the word *bias*? Because many people believe that if someone is biased, they hate "others." However, *bias does not equal hate*, despite what some people think.

Many companies put tremendous focus, time, and resources into diversity, equity, and inclusion training. That training almost always begins with discussions about unconscious bias, the unconscious beliefs and stereotypes we all have about various social or identity groups of people. Our brains attempt to categorize and organize the social world around us and the result is unconscious bias. It's normal. But the word *bias* is so loaded and perceived to be so negative that people fight it tooth and nail. They mistakenly equate it with *racist*, *sexist*, or other negative *-ist* words. No one wants to think of themselves in such awful ways, nor do they want anyone else to think of them that way, *especially at work*. Our careers, reputations, and livelihoods depend on us being well regarded at work. We feel *accused* when the word *bias* comes up, and we become very, very defensive. If we are going to have effective conversations about race at work, we have to get past our defensive reactions to the word *bias* and understand that our biases create problems in business. Our biases can turn into blind spots.

WHY BIAS MATTERS IN BUSINESS

Right now, especially if you're White, you may be thinking, "OK, if bias just means preference, not hate or prejudice, why is it such a big deal in business? Our company doesn't discriminate against anyone." It's a legitimate question. Businesses are not focused on overcoming bias because of a "Kumbaya/We Are the World" mindset. I'm betting that your company, your team, and you, yourself, truly believe in, support, and value diverse perspectives, and that's terrific. But despite that, you can still have blind spots that come from your biases, and those blind spots will hinder your success and progress as an organization. Blind spots can be tricky because you don't even know they're there. In business, they can be deadly. They can lead to poor morale, employee defection, lost customers, lower sales and profits, lack of innovation, and poor decision-making. And worst of all: You won't know about the negative impact of your blind spots until *after* something has happened. That should send chills down your spine!

Let me give you an example that will illustrate why business bias can be harmful to your organization's performance. Let's say an executive on your team is White and must hire someone for an open position. The White executive interviews two candidates who are *equally qualified*; one is White, and one is Black. The executive hires the White person. The hiring executive doesn't think, "I didn't hire that other person because she is Black," but rather, "I hired *this* person because I like her better—and the person I like better just happens to be White." That thought is, of course, happening at an *unconscious* level, which is why, in business, this is referred to as *unconscious bias* or *implicit bias*. Unconscious bias can lead to hiring more people who are just like all your other team members. It can lead to hiring the wrong person, simply because you "prefer" them, or to promoting someone who is not ready for a higher-level position.

Another potential harmful effect of unconscious bias in business is that we are more likely to side with people we prefer or like in disagreements or in decision-making. So our biases have repercussions in terms of whom we tend to favor or agree with. Again, all of this is happening at an unconscious level. We aren't aware of it when it's happening.

JUSTIFYING YOUR DECISIONS AND ACTIONS

Our brains like logic. They like it when we make sensible, logical decisions. They like it so much that they rationalize our decisions—*after* the fact—to justify the choices we make. It's called *post-hoc justification*.

Here's an example of how post-hoc justification works. A study by Yale researchers[1] found that people making hiring decisions actually *shifted* the job criteria to fit the candidate they wanted to hire. In the study, participants were asked to hire a new police chief for a hypothetical police department. They evaluated separate applications from a male (Michael) and female (Michelle) applicant. The male applicant was presented as having more street smarts, and the female applicant was presented as having more formal education. The hiring evaluators' *subconscious* impression of the female applicant was negative, but they found *logical* reasons for *justifying* that impression *after* they made their decision to hire the male applicant (post-hoc).

The study found that evaluators decided that "street smarts" were the most important trait for the position of police chief when they decided to hire the male applicant. However, when the names were reversed on the résumés in the hypothetical example and "formal education" was listed as the male applicant's strength, evaluators decided that "formal education" was the most important trait for the position, and that was the reason given for hiring the male applicant. The conclusion of the study was that people construct the criteria of merit to fit their biases as they make hiring decisions. And they will *change* the criteria to fit the decision that is ultimately made. That's weird. And certainly biased. You can see how unconscious bias leads to a decision and then post-hoc justification kicks in to validate the choice made.

So now you may be thinking, "We would probably never fall prey to that. Our company is pretty objective about hiring and key decision-making." Well, perhaps.

---

[1] Eric Luis Uhlmann and Geoffrey L. Cohen, "Constructed Criteria—Redefining Merit to Justify Discrimination," *Psychological Science* 16, no. 6 (2005): pp. 474–480.

But consider this: The same study by Yale researchers found that perceiving yourself as objective is actually correlated with showing more bias. Participants who felt most strongly that they were objective proved to be the most biased. So weird! But that's exactly the kind of blind spot that bias can create.

To cut to the chase, the study's conclusion is that our mere desire to see ourselves as unbiased is not enough to overcome decades of cultural conditioning. That desire can lead to even more post-hoc justifications. We want to think of ourselves as unbiased, so we do think of ourselves that way. But that doesn't mean we are.

Most people are good people. Acknowledging that you have biases that conflict with your values does not make you a bad person. It makes you *normal*. It's a natural result of our culture and our very basic survival trait as human beings. Remember, even babies are biased! The important thing is to find ways to *get around those biases* and eliminate them wherever you can. Blindly believing that your company or your team is a meritocracy, where everyone is evaluated solely on merit, *does not make it so*. In fact, it'll make it that much harder to address implicit bias because no one will admit it's there in the first place.

The best companies and leaders are not afraid to admit that unconscious bias exists within their ranks. In fact, they search for and identify the biases and blind spots so they can address and correct them.

CHAPTER 3
The High Cost of Bias:
Why All-White or Mostly White
Businesses Make Less Money

If your business or team is all-White, or mostly White, you may not think that's a problem, especially if you're successful and profitable. If business is good, it's easy to keep doing what you've been doing and not question whether there is a need to change your strategies and tactics. Why would you? You're successful and making money! Why would you change a thing?

But despite your success, you may be missing out on something. And you may not be able to see what you're missing because you and your team are pretty much the same and have only "one lens"—the way that you and your team view the business world is likely very similar. You don't have other perspectives or views that might challenge your thinking, create better solutions, or offer new ideas.

Here is an example of how a lack of different perspectives can cost you. Downhill skiing is a big deal. It's a multi-billion-dollar industry and employs thousands of workers. From the equipment manufacturers and retailers to the resorts and instructors, skiing is *big* business. Or it was, until the 1990s. In the 1990s, the ski industry started seeing an alarming trend: fewer skiers overall, fewer ski trips booked, fewer ski passes sold, and stagnant equipment and gear sales because skiers themselves were spending less time on the slopes. Why was this happening? Two big demographic issues were responsible:

1. The skiers themselves were *aging*. The core ski enthusiasts were getting older and that meant increased aches and pains and risk of injury. If you're 65 years old and just had a knee replacement, skiing probably isn't a sport that's high on your list.

2. The sport of skiing had continued to be one of the least diverse: 85 percent of skiers are White. Blacks comprise 14 percent of the U.S. population, but *fewer than 2 percent* of skiers. The sport is so overwhelmingly White that comedian Kevin Hart, who is Black, has an entire routine built around telling the story of when he took his family to Aspen to ski and what it was like. It's a

hilarious routine *because he makes it so*, but the stark truth of what it is like to be the only Black family on the ski slopes makes a clear and uncomfortable point.

So what did the ski industry do? Let's take these two different demographic issues one at a time.

ADDRESSING THE AGING SKIER PROBLEM

It was imperative that the ski industry find new skiers. The industry poured a great deal of money into research to learn what was keeping people from trying the sport and to identify new opportunities and customer segments. What they learned was that young people didn't really want to ski. The key reason given: "It's not for me. Skiing is what old people do—that's my parents' sport." Younger people wanted their *own* sport. They wanted to do things with their friends that were *different* than what older people do. Enter snowboarding.

Snowboarding was growing in popularity, but many ski resorts did not allow snowboarding on their public slopes! Wow—that was a big eye-opener and the biggest, most-obvious problem to solve. But that wasn't the only barrier. The research also showed that younger winter sports enthusiasts had their own ideas about the sport:

- Ski passes/lift tickets were too expensive.
- The gear and equipment were too expensive.
- The sport was too time-consuming because snowboarders had to hike up to the backcountry as they weren't permitted on the slopes.

With these consumer insights, the ski industry attacked the issues and changed *everything*: rules were changed to allow snowboarding on the slopes and at resorts. Ski passes and lift tickets became more flexible and a better price value. The ski industry worked with retailers and outfitters on extensive and creative equipment rental programs and significant price discounts to make the gear as affordable and accessible as possible.

It worked! By the mid-1990s, snowboarding had become the fastest-growing winter sport *in the world*. Snowboarding is now the focus of most young people learning an alpine sport; in fact, more than 80 percent of kids participating in alpine sports today choose snowboarding. This is significant, because it reflects the reality that the survival of any sport or industry is dependent on new users, new customers, or new participants.

But if the ski industry hadn't identified why new participants weren't being drawn to the sport, they'd have never known what the problem was and how to fix it. They knew they weren't attracting young skiers, but they didn't know *why*. It never occurred to them that young people viewed skiing as a sport for "old people" or that the equipment was too expensive. The only perspective they had was that of their core customers, who were pretty much all the same (*old*). It was only when they invited the opinions and thoughts of young people that they got an entirely different perspective.

Here is another key thing to note about this example: The ski industry *sought* the input, insights, and opinions of young people. They *asked* for their thoughts. It's not as if young people were contacting the ski industry and volunteering their perspectives. The ski industry "put the welcome mat out" for fresh perspectives and new ideas. And they got them. They listened, responded, and made changes. *The new perspective saved the ski industry.*

ADDRESSING THE LACK OF DIVERSITY ISSUE

Rob Katz is the CEO of Vail Resorts. After the death of George Floyd, he reflected on the lack of diversity in the ski industry and wrote a corporate memo sharing his thoughts. "As much as I have been saddened seeing these acts of racism across our country, I am also confronted by the fact that our Company and our sport are overwhelmingly White, with incredibly low representation from people of color. I see this as a personal failing," he said.

Katz was brutally honest and forthright—and humble—in his corporate memo. While acknowledging that the lack of diversity must be addressed and remedied, he also admitted, "I am not sure I fully know what the solution is," but he promised to "start by talking about it" with his employees at an upcoming event. His honest assessment of the problem was impressive. One of the things he addressed in his memo was the tendency to be defensive when talking about the Whiteness of the sport that his core customers so dearly love:

> *While I'm sure most everyone in our industry believes they are tolerant and welcoming, we need to acknowledge that there are parts of the culture of our sport that are clearly not inviting. Maybe the image we have created of the mountain lifestyle needs to be more varied. Maybe, as a fairly close-knit and passionate group of skiers and riders, our community carries a deep implicit bias. It would not be a stretch to call us a clique. Maybe it's our fear of change. While I would like to think that I have been an agent of change in this industry, a decade later I am still running a company that has very limited racial diversity.*

Growing diversity in the ski industry will take some time. It won't happen overnight. But it won't happen at all if the sport is not inviting and welcoming to diverse skiers of all races and ethnicities. I am encouraged by Rob Katz's candid assessment of his company's and his industry's lack of diversity and his commitment to work to do better. Vail Resorts is a huge company. It has 34 mountains in North America, and it is successful, wealthy, and the leader in the industry. Its sheer size gives it a big voice and tremendous influence. There is no doubt the steps it takes to put the welcome mat out for new and diverse customers will ripple through the rest of the industry and set the bar for its competitors.

In your business, or within your team, if everyone is pretty much the same, it's easy to miss opportunity, because *your sameness becomes your blind spot*. This is especially true if your business is successful. Doing well in business can lead to a laser focus on "what's working," rather than "what are we *missing*?"

The answer to "what are we missing?" comes from *different perspectives*. It takes someone seeing something in a different light to point out a potential problem—or opportunity. That's why having an all-White or mostly White business can cost you: You may not get a different perspective or view on business issues that could grow your sales and profits. You might not see the signs. Look at your business as objectively as you can and see if any of these signs resonate with you. If so, you're probably missing out on some opportunities that could grow your business.

SIGNS THAT YOUR BUSINESS MAY BE MISSING OUT ON OPPORTUNITIES

The following list highlights signs that your business may be missing out on opportunities as a result of bias:

- You could be, but are not, serving different populations: Black, Latinx, Asian, other people of color, LGBTQ+, different ages/generations, men, women, non-binary, disabled, and military.
- You are serving different populations, but your staff isn't diverse. There is no one on your staff who might share the perspective of some of your best customers and, therefore, no one knows how to serve your diverse customers *better*.
- You have trouble finding or keeping people of color as employees. Is it all on them, or is some of it on you? Perhaps your work environment isn't as welcoming or as comfortable as you think.
- You are not paying attention to changing demographics. As of this writing, the Latinx/Hispanic population in the United States is 19 percent of the total population, and the Black population is 14 percent. That's a full *third* of the U.S. population! It would be foolish to ignore a third of the market, but many businesses do.

If you recognize any of these signs as being valid or true for your business or team, that's a big red flag. And an opportunity! You have to get better at this to run a good business or to be a good leader.

You know that there is value in diversity from a moral and social standpoint. You wouldn't be reading this book otherwise. But business runs on metrics. It runs on *performance*. The next chapter will show you just how powerful the business case for diversity is. I call it the "diversity remedy."

CHAPTER 4
The Business Case for Diversity

Here's a fact that may come as a surprise to you: Businesses that are diverse do better in *every way* that matters in business. *No exceptions*. Study after study proves again and again that diverse businesses perform better on every metric that businesses use to evaluate success:[1]

- Higher sales
- Higher profits
- Better company reputation
- Enhanced company image
- Higher brand value
- Customer growth—in new customer acquisition *and* customer expenditures
- Higher customer satisfaction
- Greater customer loyalty
- Better customer insights and ability to anticipate customer needs
- Greater ability to attract and recruit talent
- Better quality of employee applicants
- Broader talent base with new and untapped perspectives
- Better problem-solving
- Better employee performance and productivity
- Higher levels of employee engagement
- Higher levels of employee satisfaction

---

[1] Katie Reynolds, "13 Benefits and Challenges of Cultural Diversity in the Workforce," Hult International Business School, 2019, https://www.hult.edu/blog/benefits-challenges-cultural-diversity-workplace (accessed February 7, 2021); Sundiatu Dixon-Fyle, Kevin Dolan, Vivian Hunt, and Sara Prince, "Diversity Wins: How Inclusion Matters," McKinsey & Co. report, May 19, 2020; Paul Gompers and Silpa Kovvali, "The Other Diversity Dividend," *Harvard Business Review*, July/August 2018.

- Reduced employee absenteeism
- Better employee retention
- Increased creativity
- More solutions
- Increased adaptability
- Greater innovation
- Higher market share
- A better, sharper, two-sided, competitive "edge":
  - The first "edge" that diverse companies have is that they are equipped to serve their diverse customers better. Customer service improves when staff can communicate effectively with customers from a range of backgrounds. When you have a diverse team, they bring their insights and experience to the table. They're going to deliver a better customer experience because they understand what diverse customers want and expect. A diverse team can meet those expectations and drive customer satisfaction and loyalty off the charts.
  - The second "edge" that diverse companies have is that their leadership is likely to be more diverse than their competitors, now and in the future. When your "bench of players" is diverse, as they progress professionally and become leaders themselves, they'll be less likely to overlook the customers your competitors are ignoring.

How does diversity deliver on these key metrics? What is in the "secret sauce" of diversity? The answer is one monumental ingredient: *better decision-making*. Every aspect of business is a result of decisions made: who you hire, how you train them, what products or services you offer, which new ones you create, how you reach customers and prospects, how you listen to them, how your employees collaborate (or don't), whether they feel seen and heard and valued (or don't). The entire flow of business is one decision made after another. So it makes sense that if you can improve decision-making across the board, your company or team or brand will be more successful. The enemy of decision-making is groupthink, or what researchers call the "social majority" in a company.

GROUPTHINK CAN BE POISON TO YOUR BUSINESS

We all know what it's like at work: we get together for meetings and we need to make decisions on strategy, tactics, who, how, where, and when. We go into these meetings one of two ways:

1. Engaged and fired up about the meeting topic and eager to contribute or . . .
2. Apathetic and disengaged, because "Nobody ever listens to my ideas anyway—I'm just here to get the decision and then start implementing it. Just doing my job."

In most companies, in most meetings, groupthink takes over. No one plans that or expects for it to happen, but it does: a few people kick around a few ideas or options on an approach, and after a while, the rest of the group starts nodding. This happens because the people in the meeting all agree on the topic at hand. *Or* they don't agree, but mentally "fold," because the power of the social majority of the group is greater than their own power. I'm not talking about a person's position or title within a company or about who is more "powerful." I am talking about how when people start agreeing, and those who agree become the majority in a discussion, it's easier for the rest to just go along than it is to dissent. It's hard to voice an opinion that is contrary to what the group believes and wants to do. It takes real confidence and bravery to *not* go with the flow and to speak up with an opinion or view that may not be welcome or well-received. It's easier to just keep quiet and carry on.

A disturbing result of groupthink is that when a group has been working together in the same way for a long time, the group becomes more prone to *overlook facts*. They see what they want to see, and their minds justify their decisions with thoughts like these:

- "We've always done it this way and that's what our customers expect from us."
- "We make most of our profit with this product—we don't want to mess with that."

- "We don't want to alienate any of our core customers by catering to new ones."
- "We know we need to update our approach and reach out to new market segments, but this isn't the year. We need to get our business stabilized first before we invest in anything new."

You get the idea. The *facts* may suggest that they take their business strategy in a new direction, but they ignore those facts because it rocks the boat. It's uncomfortable. And unknown. It feels safer and easier not to change anything or explore new ideas and perspectives. And that, right there, is a decision made—*and probably a bad one.*

DIVERSITY IS THE REMEDY

When a diverse group of people get together, something magical happens. Groupthink becomes harder. Why? Because people from diverse backgrounds alter the behavior of a group's social majority in ways that lead to *improved and more accurate* decision-making. They do this in three key ways:

1. They focus more on facts.
2. They process those facts more accurately.
3. They are more innovative.

When you're focused on facts and you're processing those facts accurately and without preconceived ideas or preformed opinions, innovative solutions and ideas emerge.

On top of that, diverse people bring different perspectives to the table. A team made up of diverse people will have experiences that differ, and that difference can shape their lens on issues and strategies. Their views and ideas may be fresh and innovative. Having diverse perspectives on a team can lead to innovation, and innovation leads to success. The bedrock of innovation is *diversity*—it's someone asking, "What if?" The very definition of innovation is new thinking and new approaches—the *opposite* of groupthink!

Companies spend billions each year to make their companies, products, and people smarter, better, more innovative, and more effective. Creating and working with a diverse team can achieve the same results, and it doesn't cost billions.

If diversity pays dividends—in ways that every company wants—why aren't more companies racing to make their organizations as diverse as they can be? Why do some dismiss or downplay the need to be diverse, or worse, resist it altogether?

The next chapter will cover the things people think and say and the excuses they use to avoid doing anything regarding diversity.

CHAPTER 5
The Excuses People Use to Avoid Doing Anything about Diversity

In the last chapter, I listed reasons why diversity is good for business. You would think that every CEO and president of every company and every leader within an organization would be scrambling to make their business as diverse as possible. It's a no-brainer, right? And yet excuses are made for *not* being diverse. Here are some of the most common ones and why they don't hold up in defending an organization's lack of diversity.

"There are no women/people of color in this field." *or* **"We can't find any qualified candidates."** This is probably the top reason companies and leaders give for not creating a more diverse workforce. It's true that if your company is all-White or mostly White, it can be difficult to get diverse candidates to even apply. But that means you must modify your approach and find new and creative ways to recruit. This includes widening the talent pools you tap into and marketing open positions via different avenues. Studies show that even existing job descriptions can weed out diverse candidates *before* they apply. Chapter 13 offers some tips on how to recruit great candidates from a more diverse talent pool.

Another reason this is a weak excuse is because there are often obvious channels that can create a pipeline of qualified candidates. For example, let's say you're a media outlet and you want to hire a Black journalist to ensure that you can offer readers a Black perspective on the articles and issues you're covering. A quick internet search for "Black journalist" brings up the National Association of Black Journalists, a well-established organization of Black journalists at every level, in every field, including students. That would be an obvious place to start exploring how to recruit a great Black journalist. An article in *Forbes*[1] discussed how a senior executive was complaining

---

[1] Paolo Gaudiano and Ellen Hunt, "The Top Eight Excuses That Inhibit Workplace Diversity," *Forbes*, April 10, 2017.

about a lack of qualified candidates of color and his colleague asked if he'd had any luck recruiting at HBCUs. The senior exec asked, "What's an HBCU?" The article went on to say that it's OK if most people don't know that HBCU stands for Historically Black Colleges and Universities, but it's definitely *not* OK for a businessperson who claims that they "just can't find anybody and they've looked everywhere."

"We hire for quality, not for color." This excuse doesn't hold up because most organizations don't have a clear, objective definition of *quality* when it comes to recruiting, nor do they have a methodology for assessing quality. Therefore, the assessment becomes subjective and whoever is doing the recruiting or interviewing can project their own perceptions or biases upon the process or candidate to determine "quality."

"It would be unfair to a more qualified candidate." The reason that this excuse is weak is because most hiring has *always* been tilted toward people who are known to someone in the organization or affiliated with a specific school or church. My friend Ron is in the construction industry in St. Louis. He tells me that the city is known for certain high schools that are "good" or "better" than all the others in town, and whenever they have an open position at his company, they ask candidates which high school they attended. He said, rather sheepishly, "Every time a candidate tells us they went to a specific school [one of the 'good' ones], our entire team says, 'Ahhhh, we should hire HIM!'" His team looks favorably on someone *just because of the high school attended*, even though that individual may be nowhere near as qualified as someone who attended a different school. This kind of preference happens a lot: Employees refer and recommend people they know *all the time*. Interviewers look favorably upon people who went to their same school. Or those with whom they play golf. Or attend their church. Or are referred by a friend. The point is this: Hiring has always been unfair to qualified candidates for any number of reasons.

"We already know a very good candidate in our network." The issue with this excuse is that most people's networks tend to be homogeneous. People tend to know, work with, and socialize with others who are like themselves. Therefore, tapping into your network can work *against* your diversity efforts, unless your network happens to be a diverse network.

"We promoted a woman/person of color once before and they weren't ready, so they failed." There are two reasons this is a terrible—and lame—excuse:

1. It should be obvious that one individual does not represent an entire group of people. Leaders sometimes hold diverse group members to a higher standard, and then write off the potential of the entire diverse group when the individual of that group does anything that is less than perfect.

2. People who are truly *not* qualified for a specific position should not be promoted to that position. It virtually guarantees their failure. This is tokenism and is destructive for the entire organization. People—*all people*—who are promoted to new positions should be supported because they are *new* to the position! In any new position, there is a learning curve. Promotion without support is a recipe for failure, or at a minimum, puts the newly promoted employee at a significant disadvantage.

"Our customers aren't comfortable working with women or people of color and we let them choose who works on their accounts. We can't risk arguing with them because they will just go elsewhere." Fact: People become more comfortable with diversity when they are exposed to it. That's the reason that small, rural communities often have people with more prejudiced or close-minded views. They simply aren't exposed to people who are not like them. In many small, rural areas, very few new people move in and few move out, so there are rarely new viewpoints to consider that may shape someone's perceptions or experiences. In fact, isolating ourselves from people who are different from us *diminishes trust*, and at its worst, can foster fear. The key to building diverse teams is in modeling positive behaviors and relationships—that is, leading by example. The majority group at your company can show the way by being an ally. Some companies pair an established, majority group member with a fresh face to help make diversity the norm in customer-facing roles.

"That guy is a bit of a racist, but he brings in a lot of money for the firm so we all just ignore him." Orange Grove Consulting, a well-regarded company that guides corporations and companies through DE&I efforts, has this to say about tolerating racist or toxic employees: "What they're really saying here is: We ignore bad behavior when we're afraid of losing money. Assuming that a single individual is the reason for a company's success reinforces dangerous conformity. Rarely have we heard people comment years down the line, 'We wish we hadn't got rid of Joe because he was such a producer.' Instead, they usually wish they would've gotten rid of him sooner because of his toxic behavior and influence. No one person is so valuable that they should be untouchable, but a single person can poison the entire culture if they are toxic."

"We have a work hard/play hard culture—that's just how we are. Women often don't 'fit in' here." The problem with this excuse is that it's thinly veiled discrimination. "Culture fit" is often used as a determining reason to hire a candidate or toss one out. Recruiting and evaluation processes must move away from subjective language like that and instead define, *precisely*, what a company's culture is and is not. Only then can "culture fit" be a suitable component of a candidate's viability.

"Our competitors aren't very diverse either, so our problem doesn't stand out." The name of the game in business is differentiating yourself in meaningful, valuable ways. By working to create a more diverse workforce, you'll stand apart from your competitors in a good way. It shows that your company is progressive and forward-thinking and that will align with customers who prioritize diversity. Failure to take this opportunity will make you look behind the times and out of touch. As an added bonus, you'll attract Millennial and younger workers, who not only value diversity, but expect it. This leads to even greater success, because your talent pool will be broader, and likely more innovative, than that of your competitors.

"Our company has at least 50 percent women." That's great! Wait! How many are in leadership positions? Oh, 2 percent? Hmmmm . . . Having a workforce that is half women is only impressive if those women represent the company at *all* levels, including senior leadership positions.

"What if we hire a woman and then she wants to have a baby? We need people who can focus on their work!" Wow. Hard to believe this one is still offered up as an excuse. The reality is that, other than for a very short time (when a baby is a newborn), there is no difference between male parents and female parents in terms of career attention, potential, and the need for work-life balance. This excuse reflects very outdated gender roles and is an insult to both male and female working parents. On top of that, it's likely illegal.

"The effort to grow diversity in our organization is burdensome/time consuming/expensive." Can a business really grow or make significant gains in any area (sales, customer service, marketing, technology, innovation, product development, etc.) *without* making a significant investment? I don't think so. The reason so many businesses don't succeed is that they can't—or won't—adapt to changing times and what customers want. Investing in your business is a standard part of business.

The bottom line is that diversity is good for the bottom line. No excuses. If you're a leader, you must work to educate your team or organization about why excuses like these don't hold up and why they actually foster a culture that is "diverse averse." As a leader, or aspiring leader, you'll want to make sure that you're not compounding the problem by making comments that you think are OK, but really aren't. Part IV of this book provides more specific guidance for leaders.

In the next chapter, we'll cover comments that people often make about diversity that they think make them look good, but actually make them look bad—and out of touch.

CHAPTER 6
Well-Intentioned Things White People Say That Are Hurtful or Offensive to Others

I was having dinner with my friend Quiana, and I had just started writing this book. I told her I was going to include a chapter that would tackle a list of what many well-meaning business leaders or executives say when the subject of race comes up at work. I couldn't even get past the first one on the list without her laughing her head off.

First on the list? *"I don't see color."* Quiana, who is Black, laughed until tears were coming out of her eyes! She couldn't even talk for a minute because she was laughing so hard. It made me laugh too, and I asked her, "Really? *THAT* bad? *THAT* funny?" And she replied, "Oh heavens, YES! When was the last time you were talking to another White person and they looked at you and said, 'I don't see color'? When I am talking to another Black person, we don't say to each other, 'I don't see color'! *Of course* we see color! *We all do!* If you don't see color, *then why are you mentioning it?*"

Quiana is right. And she has also heard the line "I don't see color" more times than she can count. It doesn't ring true *because it isn't true*.

People mean well. They have good intentions when it comes to diversifying their team at work. But they often say things that are untrue, weird, totally off-base, or actually offensive (unintentionally). Here are common statements that people often make when the subject of race or diversity comes up. They believe these comments are not only OK, but also make them look good. They don't. Let's take them one by one.

"I don't see color." *or* **"I'm color-blind."** *or* **"I don't care what color you are."** When people say this, what they're really trying to say is that they are not prejudiced, and they believe in the value of diversity and embrace it. And that may genuinely be true. But when someone says this, especially a leader, it's problematic, because how can you fix or improve something if you can't "see it?" To make strides on diversity, equity, and inclusion at work, you have to *not* be color-blind! You have to be able to see the inequity that exists for diverse team members and candidates. The color of our skin is one of the most obvious characteristics of all of us. If you pretend to ignore skin color or you dismiss it entirely, you minimize and negate the prejudice, bias, and racism that people of color actually experience. *A color-blind workplace is not the goal.* The goal is to create a more equitable and inclusive workplace, and we can only do that when we *acknowledge* our differences and work to create a level playing field for all.

"I treat everyone the same." Good leaders don't treat everyone the same. Your employees and team members are all unique and should be treated accordingly. For example, you may have someone on your team who excels when they are given direction and then turned loose to do the work, and you may have another who performs best when they have the chance to do a status update with you every few days. To get the most out of your employees, you need to be able to create a workplace where people's differences, experiences, talents, and skills are seen and where different needs are taken into consideration. The goal is to treat everyone *fairly*, not treat them the *same*. In fact, in order to treat someone *fairly*, you may have to treat them *differently*. For example, I worked with a graphic designer who used a wheelchair. At work, the supplies he needed for his job were placed in lower cabinets so that he could access them, and chairs in the conference room were permanently moved away from the conference table so that he could join team meetings at the conference table. Another example would be allowing personal breaks at work for new mothers to pump breast milk. In many companies, a personal break for every employee every few hours might not be necessary, but for a breast-feeding mom, it sure is. In fact, the law requires that we make accommodations for employees so that they have the ability to perform their jobs according to their needs. We are all *equal*, but we're not the *same*. Good leaders focus on treating everyone fairly.

"I'm not racist or biased." The problem with this statement is threefold:

1. The word *racist* means different things to different people. A billboard in Harrison, Arkansas, advertised White Pride Radio (the Ku Klux Klan radio station) with the message "It's Not Racist to Love Your People." Apparently, even White supremacists don't

want to be called "racist." Ibram X. Kendi, author of *How to Be an Antiracist*, says, "Even slaveholders identified as 'not racist.' It seems to me that the term is more a term of denial than a term with meaning."

2. When people say, "I'm not racist," it's almost always followed by "but." And what follows *that* is usually a pretty racist statement: "I'm not racist, but I don't understand why Black people wear braids," or "I'm not racist, but I really do think Asians are bad drivers," or "We have to raise our prices when dealing with Jewish customers, because they always chisel us down to a lower price."

3. When White people say, "I'm not racist," it can come across as hollow, because most White people don't experience racism. We tend to be oblivious. Therefore, it's hard for most Whites to understand exactly what is racist about their comments. It's not intentional, but the very statement of "I'm not racist" often has a hurtful comment or observation attached to it. For example, my friend Tamara is Jewish. Every year, in December, she will be talking with another parent at her sons' school and the other parent says, "Have a Merry Christmas!" Tamara tells me that she replies, "Thank you, we're Jewish and we celebrate Hanukkah and Merry Christmas to you!" She says that the other parent will then say, "You're Jewish? Did I know that about you? Well, that's OK." Tamara laughs it off, but she tells me she always thinks to herself, "Gee, thanks for letting me know that my religious faith is 'OK' with you. And does it change their opinion of me now that they know I'm Jewish?" The other parent doesn't mean to say anything hurtful or racist, but their comment reveals that they are oblivious and that it never occurs to them that not everyone celebrates Christmas.

Let me be clear on an important point: I am not saying that people who say any of the above comments are bad or wrong or, well, racist. What I am saying is that these comments don't strengthen your position as someone who can attract or work well with or lead a diverse group of people. They can actually tarnish the perception of you, because those statements are not *realistic*. If you say those phrases (or similar ones), you risk coming across as out-of-touch, tone deaf, or clueless regarding the *real work that needs to be done in the work-*

place. To make progress on diversity in any organization, White leaders especially must be prepared to humbly admit that they need to listen, learn, and accept that their organization or department or team has to evolve and grow in new ways.

Now that you know that these kinds of phrases don't communicate your heart or your intentions, you should scrap them. What are some positive things you *can* say that will communicate your intention and start constructive conversations? Here are sample statements that you can use to begin having conversations about race at work:

- "One of the best things about our country is its multiculturalism. But we are still not even close to where we need to be. We have inequity. While we may not be able to solve those issues, we can make progress and do better, starting right here at our company."
- "It's in our best interest to make sure that everyone in this department (or team or company) has equal opportunity to learn, grow, and advance professionally. We need to have regular, ongoing conversations about race and inequity at work, so that we can address the things we do that aren't working and come up with new solutions."
- "We say we value equality and opportunity. But we've never lived up to the promise of these. Some of us face more barriers than others because of who we are, what we look like, or where we come from. We have to recognize this and, more important, help create a company (or team or department) in which everyone lives up to their full potential. Whether we are new to this country, living in disadvantaged neighborhoods, are a different race, ethnicity, or gender than everyone else on the team, we are an 'us.' Racism and inequity affect all of us and cost us money and opportunity. Learning to talk about this involves all of us and we're looking forward to everyone's ideas on how we can do better."

Now let's move on to why your diversity and inclusion efforts haven't done the job.

CHAPTER 7
Why Your Diversity, Equity, and Inclusion Efforts Haven't Done the Job

Many companies now have Diversity, Equity, and Inclusion (DE&I) departments and/or top executives who are responsible for creating a more diverse and equitable workplace. That's a good thing. It's encouraging to see so many organizations prioritizing this and making real investments in their work cultures. Their intentions are great. But sadly, many are *not* getting the results they hoped to achieve. Their candidate pipelines aren't as diverse as they hoped. Their C-suite executives are still almost exclusively White and male. The level of engagement among associates is "meh"—OK at best. Why? Why haven't DE&I efforts to date really done the job?

Forbes identifies five big reasons that diversity efforts have not been successful:[1]

1. **Resistance:** Employees are either skeptical of their company's ability to make real change, feel victimized because they are painted as the "villain," or are singled out as a member of a diverse group. Some research has shown that mandatory diversity training can actually create *more* friction and animosity toward other employee groups.

2. **Poor implementation:** Simply *having* a DE&I program doesn't mean it will be *effective*. Many diversity training sessions have been classroom-style workshops, focused on changing behaviors, rather than changing the *inside* of an organization. For example, mentoring and sponsorship have been shown to be highly effective in creating a diverse workplace, yet these elements have been absent in some DE&I programs, particularly early ones. Employees say, "Yeah, we tried that, and it didn't really change anything"—and unfortunately, it's true.

[1]Janice Gassam Asare, "5 Reasons Why Diversity Programs Fail," *Forbes*, May 31, 2019.

3. **Lack of consistency:** Companies often implement a DE&I program after there has been an "incident," and this can come across as insincere and inauthentic, like the company is slapping a bandage on the problem just for better optics. It's like closing the barn door after the horses have gotten out. Or they do what I call "launch & abandon," making a big show of their new diversity program, but a few months later, it sputters and dies because there is no follow-through.

4. **Lack of leadership buy-in and support:** This is one of the most common challenges DE&I programs face. Early diversity efforts focused on the more humanitarian side of diversity, the "We are the world" mindset and many leaders just . . . *yawned*. Today, we know that diversity is good for business, with metrics that impress leaders and employees alike (and investors!).

5. **The "D" word:** Say the word *diversity* to some people and you can see them mentally rolling their eyes or even getting defensive. They have "diversity fatigue." I've written three books on diversity from the standpoint of business (marketing and sales, the customer experience, and leadership), and I always used the phrase *people not like you* instead of the word *diversity*. I found that people were much more open to talking about "people not like them" than they were to "discussing diversity." Early on, the "D" word just made people tune out. That's changed a lot, as DE&I programs have evolved, and companies and employees have seen and experienced the value of a diverse workplace. But the word *diversity* still alienates some employees.

Despite our progress on diversity at work, talking about race—and specifically, racism—still feels taboo for many employees. Data from SHRM, the Society for Human Resource Management, which is the premier organization for all things relating to work, employees, and workplace culture, revealed that *43 percent of American workers believe discussions about race are inappropriate at work*. Yep, inappropriate! That's a strong word. Not uncomfortable or awkward: *inappropriate*. Employees don't ever want to do anything that's deemed "inappropriate" at work! It's too risky. So the difficult conversations that need to be had have not been happening.

That's changing. Companies—and their employees—are realizing that we can't make real progress on racial equality without discussing race itself and racism. The sickening, brutal, public death of George Floyd brought into sharp focus, especially for Whites, that we are *not* all treated equally, that complaints about police brutality on Blacks are real. Eric Ellis, president and CEO of Integrity Development Corp., an Ohio-based consulting firm, put it this way: "People would say, 'Black people exaggerate the race card,' because they couldn't see it [racism]. Most people couldn't believe the George Floyd video because it was so vicious. Now they can't unsee it."

What companies found in the wake of George Floyd's death was that employees *wanted* to discuss race and racism. Employees were *not OK*. They were traumatized and needed a way to talk about their feelings and experiences. Jaime Irick, a vice president at PPG, a global coatings company, wrote a deeply personal email to the 6,000 employees he leads. He called for two things: action and honesty. Regarding *action*, Irick wrote: "We can't afford to stand on the sidelines. As human beings, we have an obligation to take an active role as to what's going on in our country." As for *honesty*, Irick said using the word *racism* is key. He stated, "I believe strongly in first embracing reality, and then defining what winning looks like. To first embrace reality, we have to use the word *racism*."

HEARING ABOUT RACISM FROM THE HORSE'S MOUTH

When you were a kid, was there ever a time when you were the last one picked for a team or a school project? It's a lonely, alienating feeling—to think that *no one really wants you to work with them or play with them*. Sure, your school or team may have made it mandatory that everyone be included, but that doesn't mean someone wasn't *picked last*. And the kid picked last *knows* that others don't really want him or her. They know that the others are *required* to include them. That's not acceptance—it's just *compliance*. What an awful, uncomfortable, self-conscious feeling that conjures up.

For many people of color, this is daily life. Made to feel last. Less than. Different. Unwanted.

At work, what must it feel like to be the only one, or the one left out of the group, or the one who is grudgingly accepted, but only because the others have to comply? You can imagine how awful that would feel to your diverse employees. You can imagine this because you're a good person and you have empathy. You're committed to making your team or your company better for diverse employees, and, especially if you're White, it starts with flexing your own empathy muscle and thinking about what *work must feel like for them*.

Articles, books, training, and classes on DE&I are terrific and necessary. But if you're White and you listen to someone of another race or background describe their first-hand, personal day-to-day experiences, it's eye-opening. Because the terrible things that happen to Black, Brown, Asian, LGBTQ+, Jewish, Amish, and Muslim (or any minority group) people just don't typically happen to Whites. We can't imagine how bad it is, or how often it happens, and we can't comprehend the chronic toll it takes on a person.

When you work with a diverse team, you have a unique opportunity to hear your colleagues' and coworkers' real stories. When they share their experiences about the things that happen to them or that are said to them, it's no longer abstract.

I think that many White people are afraid to ask about their coworkers' experiences with race, either because it's awkward or because they think that their coworkers will feel anew the pain or hurt of what they experienced. In my experience, most people are not only willing to share their stories, they're glad that someone is asking about them and wants to learn.

You have to be respectful, of course. You can't just barge into someone's office and say, "Tell me if you've ever experienced racism." Nor can you start a meaningful conversation at 2:45 p.m. when someone is prepping for a meeting that begins at 3:00 p.m. You need to choose the time and place so that a substantive and thoughtful conversation can take place. Here are a couple of examples of what starting that conversation could look and sound like.

In one-on-one conversations:

- You're having a one-on-one conversation with your colleague about their holiday plans and they share that they'll be celebrating Hanukkah with their family. The two of you are discussing what foods and activities they have planned. You say, "With all the emphasis on Christmas in our culture, does it make you feel over-looked or marginalized that Hanukkah is not given the same atten-tion? All the TV ads show Christmas scenes, and I imagine that could be hurtful and make someone who doesn't celebrate Christmas feel left out." This shows empathy because you're trying to imagine what that would feel like. If your colleague shrugs and replies, "Oh yes, it's hard! But what are you going to do?" you can ask, "I'd like to be more aware of the situations and things people say that can offend or hurt. Can we talk sometime about your experiences and feelings around that topic? Would that be OK?"

- Something horrific has happened that is targeted at a minority group or groups: a racially motivated murder or brutal beating. Or a bombing. Or extreme harassment, kidnapping, or torture. Or desecration of graves or monuments. It's all over the news. You are horrified and heartbroken and you wonder how your diverse col-league must feel. Reach out and find out. You could say, "Mario, this bombing is all over the news and it's so awful. You've been on my mind and I wanted to check in with you and see if you're OK. I'm here for you if you want to talk about it and grieve together. If you don't, I understand. I'm here for you, no matter what."

- You're in the office breakroom grabbing a coffee and your diverse colleague makes a general comment about racism or exclusion. You can say, "Shanyee, I want to be a better ally to you and other diverse people. I respect your opinions and thoughts and I want to understand as much as I can about racism and inequality so that I can do better. I want to learn. Would you be willing to talk with me about your experiences and perspectives sometime?"

In a meeting:

- A discussion in a meeting about racial inequality may be a great time to ask your diverse colleagues for their perspectives. *Or it may not.* Don't put your diverse colleagues on the spot by asking them to share their experiences. You can ask if anyone has business or life experiences to share that would help the group understand where and how your company can do better. If no one volunteers, that's OK. There will be more meetings on the topic of diversity and racism as you build your DE&I plans. Respect your colleagues' choices to share or not share.

- If someone *does* choose to share, listen without judgment or defensiveness. Personal experiences are exactly that: they're *personal*. You can't refute them; it's not open to debate. It's like someone expressing their opinion. If I say that in my experience, summer is better than winter, you can't say I'm wrong. It's my experience. It's valid because it's mine. It can be difficult and painful to listen to someone's experiences of hurt, injustice, and discrimination. Many personal stories are terrible. But they happened and those experiences leave marks on people and their lives. If someone is willing to share their perspective and experience with you, consider it a gift. It's something you wouldn't have if they didn't offer it. It should be treated with respect, deference, and empathy. Don't be defensive, dismissive, or argumentative. Don't try to minimize or justify what another person experiences.

If people feel respected and they know their experiences and stories will be treated with respect and empathy, they are usually willing to share. I think in many cases, it helps to share, to speak about experiences rather than suppressing them and not acknowledging them. When people know that your interest in them and their experiences are coming from a genuine desire to do better and be better, they are usually open to sharing.

When Irick sent his heartfelt email to his 6,000 team members, the response was swift and quite personal. Their stories poured out and they expressed gratitude for being able to really talk about their experiences. "What surprised me was how many people wanted to tell their stories," he said. Another PPG executive, Tatiana Berardinelli (human resources director, global architectural coatings), said she was *shocked* when she heard Black colleagues describe being terrified after being pulled over by police while driving. Still other Black colleagues explained how they worried about their children's safety when they left the house. "These things *never came to my mind*," says Berardinelli. Daily acts of racism happen to other people, not her.

LaTreece Butler-Morton of VMware, Inc., a California-based software company, says she thinks that her White colleagues feel that

Black people who have violently died in racist incidents are "somehow different" from the Black coworkers they see every day at work. "By sharing experiences and stories, I want them to see that it's *all* Black people who have fear, not just 'those Black people.'"

The fear that Black people live with every day is not just confined to being abused, beaten, or murdered. Subtle forms of racism are pervasive and a central thread running through the fabric of their lives. I don't believe that most White people can comprehend the daily, ongoing, *never-ending* racism that Black people—and other people of color and minority groups— experience, in ways big and small. I know I can't comprehend it. That's why it's so important for White people to hear the personal stories from people we care about and the people we work with. It's the only way that we can get a tiny inkling of what is actually happening around us.

I had a wake-up call myself on this recently. I took up boxing a few years ago. The boxing gym I go to is in a strip shopping center with a few anchor stores, including Ace Hardware, Party City, and JOANN Fabrics. My gym is located right next to the JOANN store. If I had to create a demographic profile of the typical JOANN shopper, it would be this: White woman, in her mid- to late sixties or older. That's who I see going in and out of the store every time I go to the gym.

I'm White. My boxing coach, Randy, is Black. We were talking about racism recently and Randy said that casual insults happen to him *all the time*. I asked, "Like what?" Randy replied, "Every time I leave the gym and head to my car, I can hear the door locks clicking on all the cars in the parking lot outside of the JOANN store. Those women are *afraid of me*." I was stunned. And sad. And embarrassed, because I'd never given a thought to what my coach's life is like as a Black man. I pushed back on Randy a bit, to see if he was exaggerating. I said, "C'mon, seriously? You walk out of the gym, a grown man in your 40s, dressed in gym clothes and carrying a workout duffle bag. In broad daylight. And you hear car door locks locking?" He replied, "Yes. Every day." He said it even happens to him when he arrives at the gym in the morning. He said, "I pull up in my own car and get out of *my own car* and walk across the parking lot to the gym entrance. Click, click, click—the doors lock all around me. I guess they think I'm going to carjack them."

I didn't know what to say. That's never happened to me. People aren't afraid of me. I can run my errands and go anywhere I please and never give a thought as to whether I scare someone or am in danger of being hurt. But Randy has a different experience *every day*.

The DE&I efforts and steps that companies have been taking are important. And we can build on them. But we have to do more. A key step in making DE&I progress is assessing if what you're currently doing is working and where the opportunities are to do more.

IF YOUR DE&I EFFORTS AREN'T GETTING THE JOB DONE, YOU'RE NOT ALONE

A new trend in the corporate world now is to publicly disclose the successes and shortfalls of business DE&I efforts. In the past, this information would have been kept strictly internal, but companies are now sharing their DE&I results, partly to be transparent and partly to hold themselves accountable for making real change.

At Levi Strauss & Co., 38 percent of the company's total U.S. workforce is non-White. Despite that, as of this writing, there are no Black individuals on its corporate board or among its executive leadership team. And of their top 250 executives, only 2 percent are Black (16 percent are Asian and 6 percent are Latinx).

Chip Bergh, Levi's president and CEO, wrote an open letter that was widely published after George Floyd died. In it, he stated candidly:

> *We pride ourselves on being a progressive company that takes bold stances to promote equity, justice and inclusivity all around the world—but the hard truth is that we have not always lived up to these principles internally. . . .*
>
> *It has forced us to face the brutal truth that, as much as we want to believe we've made headway in creating a more just and equal society, the data, facts and stories confirm a very different picture: we have made little or no progress in stemming deep-rooted, systemic racism. It makes me sad and angry that this is where we are as a country, but it also feels like this time is different. That gives me hope that meaningful progress can really be made.*

We also have to face another brutal truth. If we aren't actively doing something about racism, then we are an accomplice to the continuation of racism. Doing nothing is not an option. This is not somebody else's problem. This problem belongs to all of us. Saying that we stand for equality and that we reject all forms of racism is a start, for sure. But unless we put our words into action and commit to measurable progress, history has proved that we will not get very far.

The best place for us to start is with what's within our own control: our own "house." And the data, facts and stories for us internally also are very clear: we are not where we need to be. We must step up and live our values of empathy, integrity, courage and originality and fight for racial equality, inclusion and belonging, starting inside Levi Strauss & Co.

Wow. The corporate world doesn't usually talk like that. Bergh's words are so raw, real, gutsy, and honest. He takes responsibility for missing the mark and not doing enough at Levi Strauss & Co. When a leader of a global company speaks like that, it sets the bar for the rest of us. If Levi Strauss & Co. can admit its failings and shortcomings and speak to our collective role in systemic racism (and yes, we can say the word *racism*), then we can, too. We can start there, with courage and painful honesty, and a sincere commitment to do better. And be better.

Bergh's full letter announces several new ways that he plans to strengthen Levi's DE&I efforts, for all of its retail and distribution employees, as well as corporate employees. I was impressed with the transparency expressed in the letter, and Bergh's public commitment to do more and do better. You can find the entire letter here: www.levistrauss.com/2020/06/16/our-diversity-problem-and-our-plan-to-fix-it/.

Irick said that we have to use the word *racism*. I agree with him. It's not an easy word to insert into a business conversation. He said, "There are a lot of people who are unaware about racism. So if you don't call it out, my view is that you're apathetic. You can't claim ignorance. It's just apathy."

His company, PPG, is far from apathetic. It already has extensive diversity, equity, and inclusion initiatives. But conversations about racism are different from the company's other DE&I efforts, says his colleague Tatiana Berardinelli: "What we haven't done before is have these open discussions and understanding of our colleagues' experiences. We're talking about racism. *We never talked about this before.*"

In the next chapter, you'll learn why you dread the topic of race and racism at work so much and how to start a conversation centered on this topic. There is a method for doing it right, one step at a time.

PART II
How to Talk about Race at Work

CHAPTER 8
How to Talk about Race in Helpful and Positive Ways: Do's and Don'ts

Discussing race and obstacles to equity can be a very sensitive, touchy subject. And unlike other issues at work that you have to resolve and work through, this is about *people*. It's not like a software glitch, or a shipment delay, or a sales shortfall that you can tackle with a few team meetings and then move on to the next task. You have to start by talking about something that very few of us know how to discuss. It terrifies us.

HOW TO TALK ABOUT RACE WHEN—EEK!—IT IS SO HARD!

For most White people, the subject of race is incredibly uncomfortable to talk about because we have no skills in this area. We weren't taught how to do it. In fact, most of us were probably taught *not* to discuss race. The subject of race was taboo, even if we didn't understand why. Consequently, we learned to be a little afraid, or at least nervous, about broaching the subject.

While it feels weird to talk about race at work, it also feels weird to ignore it. Cheik Mboun, president of Edible Arrangements, says, "You spend so much energy working together, you can't *not* talk about it. If I'm feeling it [the unspoken tension], I'm sure others are feeling the same thing, so why not talk about it? The fear of what could go wrong is too minuscule in comparison to the fear of what may happen if people hold it within themselves."

John Page, chief corporate social responsibility officer and legal officer of Golden State Foods, a food service company in California that primarily serves McDonald's, states that the conversations that organizations need to have with their employees must convey "that we appreciate the pain folks are going through, the difficulty, the discomfort, and being honest and authentic about it."

To talk about race at work, you need to learn basic steps and then practice them to become proficient. You need a *method* that assures you are building the skills to address a necessary and difficult topic, *in a way that makes sense for business.* Chapter 10 takes you through the STARTING Method, a structured framework that will teach you how to make progress on diversity, equity, and inclusion in a way that moves your business forward. But before we go there, let's address how to talk about race in helpful and positive ways and how to handle conflict and difficult conversations about race at work.

Start with sincerity. Nothing conveys sincerity more than listening, learning, and focusing on the problem, not shying away from it. Empathy and respect are also called for, because conversations about race will bring up different perspectives and emotions from your team members. John Page states, "There will be those who are uncomfortable having these conversations and who view these discussions—consciously or unconsciously—as a challenge to the status quo." This leads me to an important point for White readers: The lens through which we view the world is not the same lens that Blacks and people of color have. Whites have not been a persecuted group or had basic rights, like housing, education, and services, denied to them. The playing field has not been a level one for everyone and it's important to acknowledge this.

Now, you might be thinking, "I can't help it if horrible and discriminatory things have happened to people of color! I can't help it if this company has been mostly White for a long time. I didn't have anything to do with that and I am being made to feel bad because I'm White. That doesn't seem right!"

Don't apologize for being White, but acknowledge that people of color are often treated differently than Whites in our society. If you're White, you have something that people of other races and ethnicities don't have. You have the luxury of *not having to think about your race much.* You've probably heard people call it *White privilege.* The "privilege" means that, for most Whites, the color of their skin has not been a problem. It hasn't kept them from living the life they choose or from professional, educational, or health opportunities. If you're job hunting, you're aware of the fact that most jobs come through personal relationships and networking. But building those networks is harder when you're not White in a majority White world. It's harder when people are suspicious of you or think you might be dangerous because of your skin color. For most Whites, the issue of race hasn't been, well, an *issue*. That's a huge (and unfair) advantage in a competitive society.

Stephanie Creary, a professor at Wharton, writes about "invisible race" and "visible race." She states that Blacks, Asians, and people of color cannot help but see race, including their own. It's visible. For most Whites, the color of our skin is "invisible." People don't treat us differently because we're White.

Liliana Ramírez, a top marketing strategist and research expert, says, "To one degree or another, the rest of us [people of color] always wonder if we or our loved ones are being judged by our work or by others' preconceptions. The feeling of being the 'only Hispanic in the room' or 'the only Black person in the room' is just not something a White person can relate to—it doesn't happen to them."

To start a productive, constructive, professional conversation about race at work, start small. I want to stress "start," because you will not just have one conversation about race at work and then "that's that," check it off your list. Race is a big, complex, layered, uncomfortable topic, which is why people are so reluctant or afraid to discuss it. Here are six ways to talk about race in helpful ways:

1. **Acknowledge the awkwardness.** A good place to start a difficult conversation is to *acknowledge its difficulty*. This validates others' feelings and "names the elephant in the room." What often happens is that the group will find a sense of relief and a welcome camaraderie in their shared discomfort. Simply say, "I've never talked about race at work before and I am unsure how to do it now. I feel a bit inept and clunky and I don't think I am going to be very eloquent. I hope you'll bear with me. I can imagine it feels awkward for you, too." You can almost hear the collective sigh of relief that would follow, because those are *honest words*. You can *trust* someone who speaks that openly and honestly. When you put it out there, in that kind of raw and unfiltered way, people can sense how real and sincere you are and *they will meet you where you are,* with their own discomfort.

2. **Find common ground.** Common ground is always there. If you look for it, you'll find it. One of the best ways to find common ground is to identify *shared values*. Even a company as large as Golden State Foods, with 68 percent of its workforce comprised

of women and minorities, starts conversations about race by agreeing on shared values. John Page states that's how they started talking about race at work, with questions like, "Do you believe in freedom? Do you believe in the pursuit of happiness?" When people agree on shared *values*, you'll find that you have more in common with them than you imagined. Common ground also fosters trust, and *when you trust someone, you can work with them.*

3. **Express sincere interest.** Without a sincere desire to do better, a conversation about race at work will likely not go well. It will come across as disingenuous and like lip service. You can't accomplish anything or make progress without sincerely being open to hearing and learning about others' views, experiences, and suggestions for improvement. Sincerity shows. Make sure your intentions are genuinely focused on creating a better workplace for all.

4. **Talk less. Listen more.** When people start talking and sharing, listen with your full attention. Don't judge their feelings. Don't interrupt to refute their experiences. Ask questions to better understand the other persons' viewpoints. Validate their emotions and show compassion. Doing so allows the other parties to speak without fear of judgment. In surveys, almost 50 percent of Black employees say they don't feel safe sharing their thoughts on race-related issues. By talking less and listening more, you'll create an environment in which people feel free to share their true feelings and experiences.

5. **Respect boundaries.** This is hard for everyone. Ask to hear about experiences, thoughts, and concerns, but don't press an employee to share if they haven't volunteered to do so. In one survey,[1] nearly 40 percent of Black employees said they feel it is never acceptable to speak out at work on the experiences of bias. Another study found that among Black professionals who aspire

---

[1] Sylvia Ann Hewlett, Melinda Marshall, and Trudy Bourgeois, "People Suffer at Work When They Can't Discuss the Racial Bias They Face Outside of It," *Harvard Business Review*, July 10, 2017, https://hbr.org/2017/07/people-suffer-at-work-when-they-cant-discuss-the-racial-bias-they-face-outside-of-it.

to leadership positions, the most frequently adopted strategy is to avoid talking about race or other issues of inequality, for fear of being labeled an "agitator."

6. **Focus on moving forward and solving a collective problem.** Acknowledge our need to do better and your sincere commitment to doing better, personally. By *our*, I mean all of us, as a society. Society is made up of individual people and you can acknowledge that you have a role in doing better and a genuine desire to do so. Again, we (all of us who are living right now) didn't create this inequity, but we can't sweep it under the rug and pretend it doesn't exist. We must acknowledge it and that the overall result of inequity is that the playing field has never been level for everyone. Keep conversations focused on strategies that can be created in the workplace that help to change that and achieve real solutions.

WHAT TO SAY, WHAT *NOT* TO SAY, AND WHY

Because it's so difficult to talk about race, especially at work, no one does it. Therefore, no one knows *how* to do it. Here are some specific do's and don'ts:

- DO be sensitive to the fact that your employees of color may not feel comfortable discussing race with you. Or even if they are, they may not *want* to. They may just want to do their jobs and get through the day.
- DON'T expect your employees of color to explain racism to you. It's not their job to help you understand racism. One friend said to me, "I didn't realize I am supposed to be the official interpreter of bias and racism for my boss. I think she thinks I am the on-demand 'Help Desk of Diversity.'"
- DO educate yourself and learn as much as you can about racism and inequity and how diverse groups are negatively affected in the business world. Broaden your lens.
- DON'T expect diverse employees to "represent" or "speak for" an entire minority population. A gay employee does not represent the entire LGBTQ+ community, a Black employee does not speak for

all Blacks, a Muslim employee does not speak for all Muslims, and a female employee does not represent all women.

- DON'T ask diverse employees how they got their jobs. It implies that some quota was in place or that they didn't earn their jobs or truly "qualify" for them. When White people get a job through networking with Whites, no one criticizes them for it.
- DO ask instead, "Tell me about your background. What were you doing prior to this role?" This is a fair and valid question and implies that the person has experience that made them qualified for the position they now hold.
- DON'T ask a person of Hispanic or Asian or Middle Eastern descent "Where are you from?" It implies that they are not a "real American" and that they are perpetual foreigners in their own land.
- DON'T comment on "how well someone speaks English." Doing so implies that you didn't expect them to speak English well because of their "otherness."
- DON'T tell Black colleagues that they are "articulate" or "well spoken." It implies that you didn't expect that they would be.
- DON'T mock someone's accent or native language. Example: Saying "Sí, señor" to someone who is Hispanic or Latinx is insulting.
- DON'T change someone's name because it's too difficult for you. I have a friend whose name is Asif and he shared with me that a client, upon meeting him for the first time, said, "I'll just call you Al." Similarly, a friend named Róisín (pronounced ro-SHEEN) said a vendor to the company she works for told her, "That's too hard to pronounce. I'll call you Rosy." Someone's name is, well, their name. Names are important and they're very personal. It's not up to you to just change someone's name and give them a new moniker. Sometimes people will offer an easier option for people they do business with—for example, "Hi, my name is Anais (pronounced Ah-nah-EES), but you can call me Anna'" But it's not up to you or anyone on your team to demand or expect that. It's a name. You can learn it.
- DO ask individuals to repeat their names if you didn't catch them the first time. It's OK to say, "Please tell me your name again." And

then listen hard so you can commit it to memory. If the name is challenging for you to say and you're not sure you'll pronounce it correctly, repeat the name back to them and ask, "Did I say that correctly?" Don't be embarrassed—some names *are* hard to pronounce. Trying to say someone's name correctly shows respect.

- DON'T mock someone's name or ask them what the "American" or "local" version of it is. Years ago, one of my coworkers, Diego, attended a client meeting for the first time. Introductions were made, and the client asked him, "What does Diego stand for?" Diego was bewildered by the question. The client persisted and said, "Does it stand for David? Or Donald? Or what?" Diego smiled and said, "It's just Diego. It's my name." The client then said, "I don't know why you people can't just have regular names." Wow. . . . "Regular" names. And "you people." Which leads me to . . .

- DON'T say "you people" or "those people." *Ever*. It implies "otherness" in a demeaning, insulting way. It's just rude. Even when wrapped in a compliment, as in "I love the way you people have such strong faith and family values," it doesn't build a bridge between people; it suggests a divide. It's *me* versus *you*. Or *us* versus *them*. What it communicates is "You're not like me" or "You're not like the rest of us."

HOW TO HANDLE FRICTION OR CONFLICT IN CONSTRUCTIVE WAYS

My friend Dana has been in a relationship with a guy for almost ten years. That's a long time. She recently told me that they have difficulty with their very different styles of money management. When I asked if they've talked about it, she said, "Oh my gosh, no! We can't. We've *never* talked about it, and we can't start talking about it now." Her comment made me think that a lot of people feel exactly that way about any kind of conflict or difficult topic. It seems easier to "let it go" or just ignore it. In our personal lives, we can choose to ignore problems rather than deal with them. But in business, if you don't deal with problems directly, they can mushroom and have significant consequences.

One of the most common issues at work is dealing with conflict of any kind. It's never easy. Now add "race" or "diversity" into the equation and conflict becomes downright uncomfortable. Here's how to manage conflict when discussing race, diversity, equity, and inclusion at work:

1. **Be prepared for conflict.** At most companies, when any new direction, strategy, or initiative is being developed, there is conflict. The bugs and kinks have to be worked out, and people don't always agree on how to do that. While discussing race or diversity may be more uncomfortable than, say, discussing a sales strategy, you should still expect that people will see things differently and have different perspectives.

2. **Reframe the conflict.** Conflict implies confrontation, and being viewed as "confrontational" at work is problematic, for you or anyone else. Move the conversation to "solution-seeking." This positively frames the dialogue, rather than negatively framing it as "conflict" or disagreement.

3. **Don't get defensive.** Becoming defensive derails the conversation, taking it from a professional issue to a personal one. It will accomplish nothing, other than to halt your collective progress. Ask yourself, "Am I trying to be *right* or am I trying to be *better*?" A more constructive approach is to say, "I want to understand your point of view. Tell me how you see it."

4. **Listen.** *Discontent* does not mean *adversarial*. Just because someone expresses that a particular aspect of your company or policies is not equitable or inclusive does not make that person "difficult" or "combative." It means *they're doing what you asked them to do*: participating in making your company better. When discontent is expressed, ask what improvements or changes can be made. Asking, "What outcome would you like to see?" is a good way to acknowledge what you've heard and drive toward a solution.

5. **Discuss; don't debate.** Not much good comes from debating someone at work. Debates drive people into different camps or "sides" of an issue. The purpose of having a professional dialogue is to discuss, ideate, explore, and collaborate. Debating

goes nowhere fast and usually solves nothing. Refocus the conversation on your *goal*, which is to develop a plan. Say, "I don't want to debate this with you. I want to *discuss* it with you. The reason we're talking about this is to *figure out a course of action*. Tell me your point of view. I'm listening and want to understand."

6. **Don't conflate or compare experiences.** Conflation is when we try to find parallels with our own experiences. If you're White, you can't draw legitimate parallels between your life experiences and those of your diverse team members. Same with comparing: Nothing will compare with the personal or professional experiences that your diverse team members have likely had. Listen to understand how they feel about their experiences and focus on what can be done at your workplace to improve.

7. **Be open to learning.** You don't have all the answers. Nor does anyone else. Collaboration is the key to identifying the challenges that exist within your organization so that they can be solved. Know that *when it comes to diversity, you probably have more to learn than your diverse colleagues*.

8. **Push the pause button if you have to.** If a conversation has gotten out of control to the point where everyone is upset, don't try to force a resolution. That's the time to pause and step away. It's in the best interests of *everyone*, so that no one says something they'll regret, which can be disastrous for someone's career. It's better to say, "I don't think we're communicating effectively now, and this is too important to not have a constructive conversation. Let's take a break and pick this up again tomorrow." This last part is important. Saying, "Let's pick this up again tomorrow" lets others know that *you're not walking away from the conversation*—you're walking away from the moment. Reflect on the conversation and what you can do to get it back on track.

Sometimes the challenge you'll face at work won't be a conflict per se. It might be that you said something insensitive or the wrong thing or you hurt someone's feelings. You're going to mess up. When you do, it's important that you acknowledge it and not sweep it under the rug.

HOW TO RECOVER WHEN YOU'VE BLOWN IT

If you're White, at some point you're probably going to say the wrong thing to a person of color or other minority group. It won't be intentional. It'll be some bone-headed thing you say because you're nervous or trying to be funny or trying to form a connection with a diverse coworker. You'll know when you've messed up, either because of the look on their face or because you *just know*. How do you recover?

- **Apologize and acknowledge.** Acknowledge that you said something out of line. Don't make excuses or try to clarify what your intentions were—it will only come across as justification. Just apologize: "What I said was out of line. It was wrong and insensitive. I'm really sorry."
- **Ask and learn.** Sometimes we sense that something we just said is wrong or insensitive, but we don't really know why. It's OK to follow up your apology and acknowledgment with a sincere question: "I know I messed up, but help me understand. Why did that offend?"
- **Keep talking and learning.** Don't let your mistake keep you from talking to people who are different from you. The goal is to build bridges so that you have a better understanding of your team's collective perspective. Keep trying. Through continued conversations, you'll learn more and be an even better coworker.

Talking about race at work isn't easy. It requires effort. But if you take it one step at a time, with sincerity and a desire to learn, you and your team will make progress. And progress feels good.

The next chapter will show you how to answer tough employee questions and what to do if an employee makes a racist remark online.

CHAPTER 9
Answers to Tough Employee Questions and Racist Remarks

Now let's tackle how to respond to three of the most common—and difficult—questions an employee may ask when you are creating and launching your DE&I efforts. Understand that these questions usually come from someone who feels resentment or doesn't agree with the language or concepts around diversity. The root of resentment is that a person usually feels that something is not fair or right. Whether an employee resents your DE&I strategy or thinks it's a mistake or unnecessary, you should be clear that you're not asking the employee to change his or her beliefs. You expect all employees to accept the direction of the company, even if they don't agree with it.

THE MOST COMMON QUESTIONS AND COMMENTS MADE BY EMPLOYEES RESISTANT TO DE&I CHANGE

"Shouldn't we just hire the most qualified person?"

Picture this: You and your team are having a meeting to discuss DE&I at your company or within your department. Everyone is mapping out next steps and action items. The topic of the meeting is how to effectively identify and recruit diverse talent for your team. The group is brainstorming on ways they can do outreach within diverse communities and how to "get the word out" that you have jobs and are looking for diverse applicants. And then someone on the team says, "Shouldn't we just hire the most qualified person?" The room falls completely silent. All eyes are on you. What do you say?

Before you respond, know that this question is a strong signal that the person asking doesn't fully understand why you're doing this. This is an opportunity to educate and reinforce with everyone that your DE&I efforts are not about "hiring minorities or people of color now," but rather strengthening and diversifying the team that serves your clients and customers. Your efforts are aimed at improving the organization as a whole with new perspectives and innovation.

A client of mine, Angie, faced this very situation recently. In a meeting to discuss outreach and recruiting, one of her employees, Samantha asked, "Shouldn't we be recruiting and hiring the most qualified person?" Angie responded in this way: "Samantha, thank you for asking that question. Let me be clear about our approach: we need to broaden and breathe some fresh air into our strategy. There are opportunities to serve our current customers better and grow our business with new customers if we understand what they want and expect. New perspectives can bring new ideas and approaches to our business that make us more competitive and innovative. We are not currently representative of our diverse community, and we need to address that, for both our short- and long-term future. Our goal is to be as smart, successful, and customer-focused as we can possibly be. We are going to hire the best people to help us accomplish this, and they may not look like you." It was a great response to Samantha's question, but what Angie said next was important, insightful, and *effective*.

Angie then said: "Race and diversity are difficult and controversial topics, and we respect the fact that some employees may not agree with every aspect of the company's new approach. We respect your freedom of thought and conscience. You are free to disagree with the company's approach, or the concept of White privilege, or structural racism, or equity. However, even if you disagree with elements of the company's approach, or some of the language and concepts we're using, we expect you to support the larger goal of increasing diversity here so we can better serve our diverse customers, employees, and prospects. This means we are asking for—and expecting—your support for our diversity efforts, even if you disagree."

Angie nailed it. She kept the door open for everyone's questions and restated the business rationale for DE&I—again. But she also acknowledged that this is new and difficult territory for many people, and she tapped into what Samantha may truly have been wrestling with: *fundamental disagreement with diversity concepts*. She didn't say Samantha was wrong or bad. In fact, she expressed that Samantha had *the right to disagree*. But Angie also made it clear that "the company has set a course and goals, and we expect your help and support as we move in this direction."

DE&I efforts must be treated like any other business goals and strategies. You wouldn't allow an employee to disrespectfully push back on sales goals, production goals, marketing direction, or branding. When a business strategy is set, employees are expected to support that strategy. If they don't, they are free to find opportunities that suit them better. As a leader, you have every right to stand firm on the way you run your company, department, or team if you've covered the business case for what needs to be done. Your job is to *get it done.*

"All this talk about race! We're all one race—the human race."

The problem with this statement is that it's very dismissive. Rather than recognizing that racial inequality is a real issue for many businesses and employees, it attempts to sweep it away altogether. It "pooh-poohs" the factual, proven inequity that exists in most businesses today and suggests that the experiences that minorities have are no different than they are for someone who is White. A good response would be something like this:

> *Phil, the majority of people in this country—and certainly the majority of people at this company—do not experience racism or know what it's like to be discriminated against. Nor do they know what it's like to be treated as an "other" or outsider, because they are the majority. While you, personally, may not have ever experienced racism or discrimination, it doesn't mean others haven't, and we are working hard to change that. Our goal here is to create a fair and inclusive workplace for everyone. That means we are focusing attention on areas like recruiting, hiring, professional development, and promotions. These areas are critical to our company's success, and just because we haven't prioritized them in the past doesn't mean that's the right strategy for where we are now.*

"I came from nothing and pulled myself up by my bootstraps. No one helped me. Why do we need to do something special for minorities?"

This is a very common question asked about DE&I efforts. People who have "made it" on their own and started with little or nothing in the way of finances and education will often ask this. And they are almost always White men. They wonder aloud why companies are doing so much now to help people of color and other minority groups "get ahead."

A client of mine, Jack, works in the construction industry. He is White. He came from nothing: his father wasn't in the picture growing up. His mom supported the family as best she could as a waitress, but she didn't make much money. They were poor. They wore hand-me-down clothing from Goodwill, never had nice or new things, and utilized food stamps for groceries (*food stamps* was the term used when Jack was a child for the program that is now called *SNAP*, the *Supplemental Nutrition Assistance Program*). They ate a lot of beans and rice. He expressed to me that this poverty left a deep and lasting impression on him. Jack got a job out of high school working for a construction company, and because he was bright and ambitious, his boss encouraged him to go to college. Furthermore, that boss made it *possible* for him to go to college: The boss found a way to have the company help out with tuition on a modest basis and gave Jack time off from work to attend classes. Make no mistake, Jack worked his butt off and it took him seven years to get his college degree because he could only take one class at a time. He doesn't understand it when people talk about White privilege. He says, "I sure as heck wasn't privileged in any way. I had *nothing*."

Jack dismisses that he has White privilege because he equates "privilege" with "money." He believes that he was not privileged because life was *not* "easy" for him. But that's not what White privilege means. It doesn't mean that your life hasn't been hard. *It means that your race isn't one of the things that made it hard.*

It's not quite so simple for people of color and other minority groups. Jack got a job out of high school. For many minorities and people of color, that first job does not happen. They may not even be considered for the job because their name is Jamal, or José, or Samir. They may not even know about an open position at a construction company because they don't know anyone in that industry or they don't have internet access at home. Or they don't know how to write a résumé. Or they can't make it to the interview because they work long hours at a restaurant and can't afford to take time off. Or they don't have a car and there is no bus route that will take them near that company's location.

After Jack got that first job, he was also privileged that his boss helped him get ahead. Now, make no mistake, his boss sounds like a terrific person. But Jack would *not* have gotten his college degree without the help of his boss. Yes, Jack worked hard and it took him *years* to get that degree. But he was "privileged" because he got some help that not everyone else gets, including that first step of "getting a job" right out of high school.

Not everyone has the same options. Not everyone is "connected" to people who can open doors for them when it comes to jobs and other opportunities. Not everyone has a name that's easy to pronounce like Jack Winter. Not everyone gets a fair shake.

For many minority groups, no one in their family has ever gone to college, or even graduated high school, because they had to start earning right away to help support their families. So they have no experience with taking the SATs and filling out applications, while other students take college prep classes and their parents hire tutors or college coaches to help them with the application exams and processes. Or perhaps the high school they went to is looked down upon because it isn't in as nice of a neighborhood as another high school. How is someone supposed to overcome that?

You don't have to feel guilty for what you have and what you've worked for. You don't have to feel "bad" for someone who hasn't had the same opportunities as you've had. But you *do* have to recognize that if you're White, in our society, you had a strong prognosis for being successful and that many people don't even have *access* to what you have. That's what "equity" means when people talk about diversity, equity, and inclusion. *Equity* is not the same as *equality*. While both words are rooted in creating fairness, *equality* means everyone gets the same treatment and level of support, in the same way. *Equity* means that fairness is achieved by giving people what they need to achieve an equal outcome.

Equality   Equity

Craig Froehle

If the question, "Why can't they pull themselves up by their boot-straps like I did?" comes up in a meeting or a conversation, frame the response in a way that opens people's eyes to the importance of *equity*. Companies today are focused on not only making their teams more diverse and inclusive, but also *making the opportunities to succeed more equitable and achievable for all.*

WHAT TO DO IF EMPLOYEES MAKE RACIST COMMENTS OUTSIDE OF WORK

Let me say upfront that I am not a lawyer, nor am I a human resources professional. Your company's legal department (if you have one) likely has clear and explicit terms for what will happen if employees make racist comments at work. The trickier part is what happens *outside* of work, when employees express their views outside the scopes of their jobs, such as on their personal social media accounts.

There are three reasons why this is such an important issue to consider:

1. More attention is being paid to racism now, and employees and customers are more likely to report an incident of racism, whether it's in-person or online. If you're a leader, you should be prepared to respond if you receive information that an employee has made a racist comment online.

2. Any racist comment made by one of your employees will hurt your business. It hurts your reputation, negatively affects your employees, and can cost you business. Most companies and customers won't do business with a company that has racist employees or tolerates racist views. That's why companies move swiftly to terminate employees who make such comments, and the termination is usually accompanied by a strongly worded press release, fiercely denouncing the employee's comments or actions.

3. You're trying to do better and be better. You're reading this book to learn how to make your company, department, or team as inclusive, diverse, fair, and welcoming as you can. The words of a racist employee contradict your corporate values and can negate your DE&I efforts.

What about free speech? Don't people have the right to speak their minds? Especially when it's on their own social media accounts? Yes and no. In the U.S., we have have freedom of speech, but there are limits. It is not legal to yell, "Fire!" in a crowded theater, nor is it legal to threaten someone. The First Amendment gives us the right to express our beliefs, but the First Amendment does not prohibit an employer from terminating an employee for saying something the employer does not like, even if the speech occurs outside of the employee's work hours. The Constitution's right to free speech only applies when the *government* is trying to restrict it, not a private business.

If an employee makes a racist statement online, *don't ignore it*. Look into it promptly and consult with your legal counsel to determine whether terminating the employee is within your employer rights. Once you've been advised of the proper course of action and have taken that action (e.g., discipline, "writing the employee up," or termination), follow up with a company-wide communication that addresses the situation, why it will not be tolerated, and what steps the company has taken. Use this communication (an email or a meeting) to restate your corporate values and your commitment to demonstrating those values in the way you work each day. Your employees need to know that *treating people with respect is part of their job description* and *a requirement of your company*, and that if their behavior has even the *potential* to harm your company, consequences will follow.

CHAPTER 10
Where to Start When You Don't Know Where to Start: Eight Steps to Making Progress on DE&I

Have you ever thought about all the things you've learned to do that began with the most basic, simple, fundamental steps? Here is a list of things we all had to learn how to do that may have seemed difficult at the time, but we have become so proficient at them now that we can do them with barely a thought:

- We learned how to read. We started by learning the alphabet, and perhaps we learned the alphabet by "singing our ABCs." We then learned the sounds those letters make, and we learned how to assemble those letters into words and those words into sentences.
- We learned math. We started by learning numbers and then learning to count. We then learned how to add and subtract, multiply and divide. We learned fractions. Then algebra. And some of you (not me!) learned complex math, such as calculus.
- We learned how to drive. We started with coursework that taught us the rules of the road and what all the road signs and traffic signals mean. We learned about auto safety. We learned about acceleration and braking. And then we got behind the wheel and learned how to drive on roads, merge onto freeways, and parallel park.

You get the picture. *Everything* that you have *ever* learned to do started with basic steps that culminated in proficiency.

Talking about race at work is like that. Just because you've never had a conversation about race at work, or you've only had limited conversations, doesn't mean you can't *learn* to do this. Like anything else you're trying for the first time, it may seem daunting and you may feel clunky doing it. That's OK—it's part of the process.

Now, let me be clear: I am not equating the challenges of deep discussion about race at work with learning to drive or learning how to read. I am simply painting a picture that most of the skills that you have are *acquired*. You weren't born with them. You were taught and you learned. You made mistakes and learned even more. You tried new approaches. Some worked; some didn't. You *kept trying*, learning more and more, advancing and refining your techniques, until you *got comfortable with your proficiency*. And then performing that skill or task no longer freaked you out. My method for tackling the subject of race at work will take you from beginner to proficient in eight simple steps.

Keep in mind that *simple does not mean easy*. The STARTING Method below is simple, but it's challenging. The fact that you're reading this book tells me you're not afraid of a challenge. You're not afraid of doing the work, even difficult or complex work, to get the reward. You know that making your workplace more diverse, equitable, and inclusive is worth the effort because it *really matters*.

THE STARTING METHOD

This method uses the acronym STARTING, not only to aid in the understanding and recall of the steps, but also because DE&I efforts are never "finished." STARTING stands for Sincerity, Transparency, Acknowledgment, Respect, Tools, Investment, Nurturing talent, and Goals. My method has been developed by experience, study, trial, and error—and a *great deal of input from highly qualified experts* who teach organizations and corporations of every size how to make progress on DE&I. But true diversity, equity, and inclusion in the workplace is in its infancy. We will always be "starting." And the best way to start is with sincerity.

Sincerity

The STARTING Method begins with *sincerity*. You won't get very far in creating a better work culture if you don't believe that it's an important endeavor. If you're doing this because you "have to," or because you're under pressure to be "politically correct," your efforts will not be as effective as if you are genuinely striving to make meaningful change. People can sense sincerity—and they can sense insincerity, too. If your heart isn't sincerely into making your company, department, or team better by doing better, your efforts will come across as disingenuous, exploitative, patronizing, and empty.

But I know that's not the case with you! You are reading this book and educating yourself on how to be better and do better. However, you may face others at work, either above you or below you, who do not believe that DE&I progress is important or necessary. In those cases, you will have to work to convince them that people can instantly spot insincerity and that it's not in the best interests of your organization to spend time, money, and effort on an issue that is viewed as gratuitous or "window dressing."

Even if you don't say everything perfectly or smoothly, your sincere desire to start the conversation and talk about DE&I will show. Trust me on this. It is amazing how people respond to true, heartfelt efforts, even if they're a bit clunky. As a White woman, I have found that when I have questions about race or inequity issues, and I ask diverse colleagues for help or answers, they more than meet me halfway. They go the extra mile to help me understand or to provide a perspective that I lack. Never once has anyone said to me, "How dare you ask me about that! I am not helping you!" In my experience, people *want* to build bridges. We want to come together and better understand each other. If you have a sincere and genuine interest in learning how your workplace or team can do better, you'll find that people will go out of their way to help you.

Transparency

Be real. Be honest. Even about your own apprehensions. It's better to grapple with the difficulty of discussing racial inequity than to say nothing at all. It's OK if you admit that you've never done this before and you don't quite know how to talk about this. Your team can probably sense that anyway, so you might as well be upfront about it.

For example, let's say you're pulling together a meeting to discuss how to do a better job with DE&I at your company (or in your department). You could say the following to your team, either face-to-face or in an email:

> *We haven't done as much as we need to on the issue of diversity in our team (or XYZ Company). It's time that we address this and do better. While I don't know what*

the path forward is, I know it starts with all of you, and all of us. We need everyone's voice and everyone's help to identify the areas that we need to fix or improve and build the team we are capable of being. Please join me for this important meeting to start the conversation, discuss ideas, share thoughts, and establish goals moving forward.

In this example, you, the initiator of the meeting, have openly shared that (1) as a team, you haven't done as much as you could; (2) you don't know what you should do or what to do first (the path forward); and (3) you need help.

- It's important that your team understands that you're asking for help from *all of them*, not just your minority team members. It's not your diverse employees' responsibility to fix or improve areas in your organization. When it comes to making your workplace more diverse and inclusive, you'll want *everyone's* help and insights.

Being candid and transparent about what you don't know, about what you're concerned about, and that you can't do it without help is a great foundation for having a meaningful conversation on this sensitive topic. It shows that you're willing to be vulnerable because you don't have the answers and, if you're White (or straight or male), that you know you don't have *the needed perspective*. It lets others know that they, too, can express their own apprehensions or concerns. It sets the tone for "real talk" and is essential for building trust and having tough, but truthful, conversations.

Acknowledgment

Whether you're leading a team discussion or participating with co-workers in a discussion, it's crucial to acknowledge the uncomfortable realities of the past and the present. For example, did you know that a résumé with a Black- or Asian-sounding name gets *half as many call backs for interviews* than one with a White-sounding name? In fact, discrimination based on one's name or belonging to a particular group is so prevalent and well documented[1] that diverse applicants have a name for shielding their race on their résumé: it's called "Whitening a résumé." Different minority groups use different techniques to do this. For example, Asian applicants often "Americanize" their names (e.g., changing "Lei" to "Luke") and do the same with hobbies and interests, including outdoorsy activities like hiking and kayaking. One Asian woman said, "I don't want anyone to think there could be a language barrier. You can't tell I speak perfect English from my résumé. I can demonstrate that when I get the interview, *so I have to be able to get the interview.*" Many Black applicants will change not only their name, but drop the word *Black* from their professional organizations (e.g., changing "Society of Black Engineers" to "Society of Engineers"). One Black college senior stated, "People want to have an awesome Black worker, but they want one who they feel fits within a certain box. I feel like race is one of the many aspects where you try to just buff the surface smooth and pretend like there's nothing sticking out."

For women, the business snapshot over the past six years has changed little, with minimal progress on pay equity and advancement to management and leadership. And for Black women, the situation is worse: They are promoted more slowly than other groups of employees and are significantly underrepresented in senior leadership.[2]

There are a zillion examples of inequity, injustice, discrimination, and wrongdoing. The bottom line is that to make meaningful progress on DE&I in the workplace, you have to start by acknowledging that the terrible truths and reality of the past were not experienced by most White people. You have to face these truths and acknowledge them to get to the next level of productive communication and human connection.

---

[1] Dina Gerdeman, "Minorities Who 'Whiten' Job Resumes Get More Interviews," *Harvard Business School Working Knowledge*, May 17, 2017, https://hbswk.hbs.edu/item/minorities-who-whiten-job-resumes-get-more-interviews; Janice Gassam Asare, "Are Job Candidates Penalized for Having 'Ghetto' Names," *Forbes*, February 20, 2020, https://www.forbes.com/sites/janicegassam/2020/02/20/are-job-candidates-still-being-penalized-for-having-ghetto-names/?sh=224ac9ef50ed.

[2] Sara Coury, Jess Huang, Ankur Kumar, Sara Prince, Alexis Krivkovich, and Lareina Yee, "Women in the Workplace 2020," McKinsey & Company report, September 30, 2020, https://www.mckinsey.com/featured-insights/diversity-and-inclusion/women-in-the-workplace.

Respect

Respect is powerful. It can move mountains. Respect underscores and amplifies the sincerity and transparency that you bring to the table to make progress on DE&I at work. Before I share ways in which you can demonstrate respect to your coworkers and team, here are four reasons why respect is so effective in bridging differences between people:

1. Respect acknowledges a person's *basic human value*. It conveys that we all deserve to be treated with kindness, fairness, and dignity. From a workplace standpoint, respect honors a person's experiences, perspective, talent, and accomplishments.
2. Respect communicates *acceptance*. When we accept someone for who they are, *even if they are different from us or we don't agree with them*, it fosters trust. Coworkers and teams must be able to trust each other to be effective at work.
3. Respect creates an environment in which people feel *safe to express themselves*. This is critically important for any business, because innovation and breakthroughs for better business approaches come when team members feel safe enough to explore new ways of thinking or working and safe enough to try new things.
4. When we feel respected, we feel *seen and valued*. When I was about eight years old, I got a modest allowance that I was allowed to spend any way that I wanted. My friend and I would go to the neighborhood drugstore and buy gum or candy or comic books. When we would go to the cashier to pay, many times an adult customer would approach and start putting their items on the counter, even though we were there first. We learned to step aside and let the adult go first, not out of respect, but because they were bigger and they "mattered," and we were kids and "didn't matter." This feeling of "not mattering" was reinforced by the actions of the cashier, who would just start ringing up the adult customer's items. But one day, as I was putting my gum on the counter to pay, an adult woman hustled up next to me and began unloading her basket of items on the counter. She pushed my gum to the side to move her items forward and started reaching

for her wallet to pay. The owner of the drugstore was working as the cashier that day and he looked at me, looked at her, and then said, "Ma'am, this girl was here first. Let me take care of her and then I will help you." The woman was angry! She muttered and harrumphed and glared at me. She assumed her "adult-ness" overrode my "kid-ness." And I had always assumed the same thing! The store owner took his sweet time in ringing me up, chatting with me for a moment, and carefully putting my gum in a paper bag for me. This story sounds so silly and inconsequential, but I vividly recall the way it made me *feel*—like I *mattered*. It made me feel that, although I was a little kid with my little purchase of gum, I was seen and I was valued. The owner saw me as a legitimate and *equal* customer, even though I wasn't spending very much. I felt so validated!

Seven Ways You Can Show Respect to Your Diverse Team

Respect is profoundly meaningful, but *costs nothing to give*. Here are ways you can demonstrate (and model) respect for your diverse co-workers, regardless of who they are or what their positions are within your organization:

1. **Listen without interruption, arguing, or defensiveness.** This may be the most important—and easiest—thing you can do. When working with people who are different from you, actively listening to their ideas, feedback, thoughts, or concerns conveys tremendous respect. Give them your full attention and let them finish speaking before you comment or ask a question.

2. **Ask questions.** Questions are respectful because they encourage someone to share their opinions, ideas, and input. When talking with team members, particularly about difficult subjects such as race or inequity at work, we are often uncomfortable asking questions, because we don't know where the answer will lead. And we're uncomfortable with the conversation as a whole, so we sure don't want to prolong it by asking questions—we just want it over with! But asking questions such as "Can you tell me more about that idea?" or "What are the obstacles we need to

identify to address this?" or "What do you think is the best way to proceed?" are not only viable, they also convey that you're *committed*. You're *in this,* and you're not afraid to learn more.

3. **Honor their experience, instead of discounting it.** Whether it's professional experience or life experience, your diverse team comes to the table with experience you probably don't have. It could be very positive experience, but it may not be, and it's important to acknowledge their experience, regardless of whether you can relate to it or fix it. For example, my friend Tasha is a Black woman who worked in a warehouse when she was in her twenties. She was the only woman on the team, the only Black person on the team, and the only one in her twenties. All the guys were White and had at least ten more years of experience. She wasn't harassed in an overt way, but the team found ways to put her down or dismiss her capabilities. When she would bring up an issue or problem she'd come across, the guys would say things like, "Don't you worry about that, missy—just finish the report and leave the problems to us." She felt she wasn't learning and growing much in that role, so she resigned and took another job. On her first day in her new job, her manager met with her for an hour and asked her in-depth questions about her past experiences, saying, "We are so excited about having you on our team. The first thirty days in any new job are a big learning curve, and I want to get you off to a strong start. I'd like you to tell me about how you learn best, what blocks progress for you, and what support I can provide that will be helpful to you in the next thirty days." Wow! What a great "first day on the job" conversation! Anyone would feel supported and respected and valued with a conversation like that! With that foundation of respect and trust, from day one, Tasha felt comfortable and safe to share her experiences from her previous job, good and bad. And her manager had a better understanding of what would help her be successful from the start. Tasha and her boss enjoyed a fabulous working relationship for more than a decade and she credits him with showing her exactly how to demonstrate respect and support for an employee.

4. **Validate their contributions.** We all like to be recognized for our contributions at work. It feels good to have others comment on our work, our commitment, and our expertise or experience.

By validating a coworker's contribution, you show respect for their efforts—and the outcome. Jonah is an IT professional at a large manufacturing company. In manufacturing, production equals money and downtime equals lost money. When the company went through a major software and systems upgrade, he worked for six weeks straight without a single day off to ensure that the upgrade process went smoothly and the manufacturing pace continued without interruption. His boss not only congratulated him on the success of the installation, but also praised him in an email *to the entire company*. Jonah was also invited to a meeting with the company's top executives, where they thanked him for his tireless efforts and his dedication to making sure the manufacturing process continued uninterrupted. You can imagine how good Jonah felt about his work and the respect his company and his boss showed him for his contribution.

You don't have to wait for a "big moment" or a monumental achievement to validate someone's contribution. Some of the most significant contributions workers make are the smaller, steady, everyday ones that keep business moving forward. Let's say you have someone on your team who prepares a monthly budget report. It may be a task, but it's an important one. You can show respect for that employee's ongoing contribution by telling them, "In the budget forecast you create each month, I want you to know that I see how much care and detail you put into it. It's evident. It's very thorough and that's critical to the planning process. I wanted to specifically let you know that your attention to detail is very much appreciated and valued. Thank you for always doing such a terrific job on that." Wouldn't a comment like that feel good? *Everyone* likes recognition and respect for the work that they do.

5. **Avoid teasing.** Some people say that teasing is a sign of affection. After all, as an adult, if you don't like someone, you *don't* tease them—you *ignore* them. But at work, it's best to avoid teasing someone because you may not know when you cross the line from playfulness to mocking. What you consider playful joking could actually embarrass or hurt someone and you might not even know it.

6. **Don't blame. Focus on constructive outcomes.** Blame doesn't work very well when it comes to solving a problem for two reasons: (1) it's disrespectful, and (2) it is rooted in the past.

- Blame typically makes the other person defensive or forces them to admit to making a mistake. Admitting to making a professional mistake is quite embarrassing and, in many cultures, it is profoundly shameful. It's better to address a mistake or problem by talking with the individual about what happened, identifying where the breakdown occurred, and then moving to, "What can we learn from this and do differently so that this doesn't happen again? What needs to happen to get this back on track?" This approach puts the mistake on the table for examination and discussion and respectfully identifies that the worker is responsible (because it's their job), but *preserves their dignity*. It allows them to step up and fix their mistake with their pride intact.

- Blame is focused on what already happened and an outcome that already occurred ("How could you let this happen?" or "Why didn't you tell me the project was over budget?" or "Why didn't you finish the sales report yesterday?"). It's *very* important to identify how mistakes are made or where processes break down, but it's more respectful and productive to focus on a *better future outcome and getting it right* than to focus on the past with blame.

7. **Respect boundaries.** We all have boundaries, but some people are not good at saying no. It can be especially difficult for a worker to tell a coworker or boss that they are uncomfortable with a request. It's hard to tell someone to back off, especially someone in a higher position in your organization. Show respect to your coworkers by not overstepping their personal or professional boundaries.

- Here are some common ways that boundaries get abused at work:
  - Asking single or childless workers to stay late to finish a project or meet a deadline because those who are parents have to get home to their kids.
  - Asking people who are bilingual or speak multiple languages to translate for you.

- Expecting women to choose between their family and a job promotion that requires long hours and/or business travel. It's not an "either/or"—and it's not your business. Many, many women successfully balance family and demanding jobs and travel for work. Rarely is a man asked whether a job promotion will interfere with his family life. It's not your job to determine what another person can handle regarding their work and home life.

- Expecting people of color to "speak for" or represent their entire race or ethnicity. I don't speak for all White people. Or all women. How could I? People who have kids don't speak for all parents. Someone who lives in California doesn't speak for all residents of the state. You get the idea. While it's wise to get input and perspective from your diverse team, it's unfair to put pressure on them to come up with solutions or processes just because they're Black or Brown or Asian, etc. They're employees, not sociologists. The same is true of expecting a gay employee to "speak for" or represent the entire LGBTQ+ community.

Showing respect to people of other races, ethnicities, gender or gender identification, cultures, and generations is the foundation of having productive conversations about diversity, equity, and inclusion at work. You're trying to make your workplace better, but you can't do it alone. You need help from the diverse people you work with each day. They'll help you get it right if they know that you're coming from a place of respect and sincere interest. Respect is the key that opens the door to real talk and real progress.

Tools

Your employees and coworkers are going to need tools and skills to navigate conversations about diversity, equity, and inclusion. They'll especially need tools to talk about race within those conversations. Tools and tactics serve three purposes:

1. They serve as a framework for employees of what to do—and not do.

2. They provide the employer a structure that is tested, shown to be effective, and compliant with laws and corporate policies.
3. They remove the subjective and personal aspects of DE&I conversations and replace them with objective and business-driven dialogue.

Providing practical, accessible tools and training is essential. Your team has to feel that *they can do this*. Chapters 11–18 cover specific tips and tactics for dealing with a myriad of questions and issues about race and diversity issues. Additional resources in the areas of corporate training, consulting, and human resources are included in the Appendix.

Investment

In Chapter 5, we covered the main excuses that people use to avoid doing anything about diversity. One of the excuses was "It takes too much investment." In the STARTING Method, the investment step can be interpreted as time, capital investment (money), or resource and talent investment (people). For large corporations, the investment will likely be all three of those. For a small business, investment in making DE&I progress will most likely be one of *time*: you'll need to devote time to following the steps, tracking your progress, and refining and honing as you go.

The key point of this step is to state clearly that making improvements to DE&I requires investment. It won't just "happen." Like any other part of your business that you want to improve, it must become a priority. That means you can't dabble in DE&I in your "spare time" or expect changing demographics to automatically work in your favor. You have to set goals, identify opportunities, and make DE&I a focus of your ongoing business plan.

Nurturing Talent

This may be the most important step in the STARTING Method. Because if you do all the other steps—you sincerely, transparently, and respectfully work with your team to build a more diverse workplace and invest the time and money to create real change—but then you neglect the talent you've worked so hard to find, recruit, and hire, you won't get the results and benefits of a diverse team. Your talent will likely chug along, plugging away at their jobs and getting things done, but they may not *soar*. When workers are nurtured, they flourish. They perform exponentially better and their productivity, engagement, job satisfaction, and retention skyrockets. As an added bonus, employees who feel their careers are nurtured are more likely to recommend, refer, and bring in other great employees, too. They become ambassadors for your business or your department.

Now, the word *nurture* may sound a bit gooey to you, like you have to "baby" your employees. You don't. Nurturing talent is about knowing your team and enabling each person to *fulfill their potential* by allowing them to play to their own strengths. It's not only about their professional development, but also about making sure they have the opportunities that will help them get to the next level and succeed overall.

Nurturing talent is an *ongoing journey*. It's most effective when it consists of a mix of appropriate training and opportunities, mentoring, and networking opportunities. It's a journey you take *with* an employee, together. It's so important and instrumental to people's success that Chapter 14 is devoted entirely to how to nurture your diverse talent effectively.

Goals

Business runs on goals: sales goals, profit goals, management goals, customer service goals, product development goals, and more. You can't track your progress on anything if you don't know what you're measuring it against. Setting clear goals is imperative to assess where you're hitting the mark and where you're missing it. Effective goals are comprised of three factors:

1. They must be specific.
2. They must be achievable.
3. They must be measurable.

Making progress on DE&I is a journey and an evolutionary experience. You'll learn things along the way that may alter your route. You'll try things that work and discover some that don't work. You'll tweak, adjust, and do course corrections. You may abandon some tactics in favor of others. But it all starts with having specific goals that are *specific*, *achievable,* and *measurable*. There's a common phrase in business that "if you can't measure it, you can't manage it"—and it's true.

In Chapter 7, I shared the open letter that Chip Bergh, Levi's president and CEO, posted about the awakening he had regarding making true progress on DE&I. What greatly impressed me about that letter is that he went further than admitting that the company could do more. *He put a stake in the ground.* Within that letter, he got real—and *specific*—about exactly what steps the company would take to improve DE&I and he spelled out, for all the world to see, the specific goals that were set. To illustrate the breadth of those goals, and just how iron-clad specific they are, here is the portion of his letter that listed the company's goals:

We will be transparent about our progress, publishing annual updates on our employee demographics and diversity statistics.

- Building on the pay equity studies we did in 2018, we will run and publicly publish wage equity audits every other year, starting with a U.S. study in Q4 2020, with the goal of expanding globally.
- We will reinvigorate our search for a Black leader to join our board of directors, adding to a cohort that includes women and people of color.
- We will achieve meaningful, year-over-year improvements in our diversity metrics. We will do this by updating our recruiting and retention strategies to diversify our talent pool.
  - We will strive to have Black, Latinx, Asian, or other minority representatives be half of interviewees for open positions.
  - We will expand our leadership and development opportunities for women and non-White employees with our RISE Leadership Program in LSA and LSE and our Denim Tribe program in AMA.
  - We will continue to partner with historically Black colleges and universities and diverse campus organizations to increase recruiting efforts with underrepresented populations.

- By 2021, we will launch a career path program for retail/distribution center employees who aspire to join the corporate team so we can nurture and promote the diverse talent that already exists throughout our company.
- We commit to creating a more inclusive culture where everyone feels welcomed, heard, and valued.
- We will commemorate Juneteenth as an annual paid holiday globally. Although generally a U.S. holiday—it marks the day in 1865 when Union soldiers landed in Galveston, Texas, with news that the American Civil War had ended and all enslaved people were free—we will work with our teams around the globe to determine how best to implement it locally in a meaningful way.
- We will train all of our employees on anti-racism and racial equity. We'll launch this training this year and ensure everyone completes it by the end of next year.
- Our ERGs (Employee Resource Groups) have already changed the conversation at the leadership level, shaped policies and influenced product and marketing in the short time they've been up and running. So we will expand our ERGs to more geographies in 2020 and continue to invest in these groups.
- We will complete a thorough and comprehensive review of our workplace policies to ensure ethnic, racial, and gender equality in our workplace.
- We commit to continuing to use our voice to advocate for change at the policy and community levels.
- We will continue to stand up for government programs and policies that advance equality, address systemic discrimination, and improve conditions for communities of color and underserved people.
- Over the last five years, our company and the Levi Strauss Foundation together have invested more than $37 million in organizations advancing social justice and equality in the U.S.

- We know change happens at the ballot box. We will continue to support voter registration and education for employees and consumers and are aiming to sign up 1,000 companies to Time to Vote, an initiative we helped establish to ensure employees can take time away from work to vote. This year, the Levi Strauss Foundation is making $1 million in grants to support get-out-the-vote efforts and voting rights in the United States. These efforts are even more important now as the pandemic has led to longer voting lines, fewer poll workers and disproportionate barriers to voting for communities of color.
- We will leverage our corporate grantmaking, employee giving, volunteerism and civic engagement programs to activate employees to support racial justice organization and be part of the change.
- Change will not occur unless we hold ourselves accountable. I welcome your ideas and feedback, and I hope you speak up if you don't think we're keeping our promises. It's going to take all of us to make a difference. We all must step up in this fight for change.

This list is extensive, covering everything from a specific percentage of diverse candidates for interviews, to commemorating Juneteenth as a holiday, to time off so that employees can vote. They even set a date for launching the career path program. That list is comprised of big goals! But even big goals can be tackled and achieved if they are specific. Without specific goals, you have no real way to know what you've really accomplished. It's like driving around without a destination or a map. You're just driving, taking in the scenery. Specific goals let you know *where you are* on the journey and *how close you are* to reaching your destination.

If you're a small to mid-sized organization, here are some examples of goals that may be realistic for you and your team and initial steps to take to achieve them:

• Make a commitment to seek qualified diverse candidates for your open positions. You can't hire diverse talent if they're not even in the recruiting and interviewing pipeline. Get specific with a goal of having diverse candidates comprise 50 percent of those interviewing for an open position.

- Broaden and diversify your network. For example, if 30 percent of the population are White men, but 90 percent of your LinkedIn connections are White men, it's time to focus on broadening your contacts and your network. Set a goal to add fifty new, diverse connections in a year. Join diverse groups online to accomplish this.

- Do outreach to form alliances with diverse professional organizations. For example, a small law firm can develop a relationship with the local Black or Women Attorneys Association. Set a goal to identify and connect with two organizations.

- Review the skills you need for specific positions and widen your thinking when it comes to job promotions. Sometimes specific industry skills are required, but many times, skills in one area can transfer to an entirely different area. Look for comparable experiences as well as transferrable skills. AbeTech, a mid-sized Midwestern company that helps businesses simplify their technology systems, uses this approach with their employees. Chris Heim, AbeTech's president, says, "We look for *how* an employee can contribute and succeed in our company. If a person is good at X, where else do we need that skill? Our employees love it, because they don't feel pigeonholed into one role or department within the company. If a position calls for an innovative problem-solver, who do we have who does that well? If we need someone to be a strong liaison with one of our partners, who on our team demonstrates that skill set?" This approach brings *diversity of thought* to your organization, which drives innovation.

Now that we've covered the STARTING Method and you understand the steps, let's move on to how to build business relationships with people who are different than you.

PART III
Making Diversity, Equity, and Inclusion Real

CHAPTER 11
How to Build Business Relationships with People Different Than You

The beer industry is huge in Colorado; there are more than 400 independent craft breweries throughout the state. While each has its own personality and vibe, and the beers they brew are their own recipes and flavors, there is one thing that almost all of them have in common: they are owned by White men. Beer brewing is one of those industries that attracts a lot of men to it and most of those men happen to be White. In fact, there's even a good-natured joke about it: "Craft brewing—the hobby for straight, White men." But Atrevida Beer Co. in Colorado Springs is breaking that mold and stereotype.

Atrevida bills itself as a "female-forward, Latin-inspired brewery." The company is owned and run by married couple Jess and Rich Fierro. Jess is Colorado's first female and Latina brewery owner and head brewer. She's won numerous awards for her business and her beer, and she was the *winner* on Season 1 of *Beerland*. Jess really, really knows beer. She also knows what it's like to be a minority in her industry. In fact, Jess is a "double minority": she's a woman *and* she's Hispanic. There aren't many women who are brewers, and Jess and Rich don't know of a single other Latina who brews professionally. Their Mexican heritage, traditions, flavors, and foods inspire many of the beer recipes that Jess creates.

They've created a unique niche for themselves in a very crowded business space. New breweries open every week, and many don't survive the highly competitive market and saturation of breweries. Atrevida has been in business since 2017 and each year, its business grows. There are several reasons for this, starting with a great product and, of course, running the business well. But Jess and Rich attribute much of their success to the defining principle of their business: diversity. They believe so strongly in the power of diversity that the brewery's tagline is "Diversity: It's on Tap." The signage for their business features two large signs: one with the Atrevida brewery name, of course, and one with "Diversity: It's on Tap." But here's the kicker: The sign for their tagline is as large as the sign that has the name of the brewery. They make it clear that everyone is welcome at their brewery.

When George Floyd was killed by Minneapolis police officers, Jess and Rich were moved to make a statement that their business stands with diversity. They made their website all black the next day, with just the words *Remember George Floyd*. It was their quiet way of showing solidarity for those who were grieving and waking up to a moment of reckoning. Then an interesting thing happened.

A woman from the Black Latino Leadership Coalition of Colorado Springs contacted Jess. (Colorado Springs is *not* a very diverse area at all. The local Black and Latino communities have joined together as one coalition because they have mutual goals and can accomplish more by working *together* than independently. Brilliant.) Although Jess knew of the coalition, she wasn't involved in it. The woman introduced herself to Jess, said she'd seen their blacked-out website page, and thanked Jess for her support. She told her she wanted to host an event on Juneteenth, to educate the community about the date's significance and celebrate the date. Juneteenth, June 19, is the day that commemorates the end of slavery in the United States.

The woman asked if Jess would be willing to brew a special beer in honor of Juneteenth. Jess agreed and went to work, tirelessly researching the food and drink that slaves consumed in celebration on that day. She learned that the common celebratory drink was a specific type of cream soda and that the foundational flavor of that soda is vanilla. Jess created a special beer using vanilla and other flavors that featured significantly in the Juneteenth celebratory foods.

Jess and Rich also offered their brewery space as the place to hold the event. The woman from the Black Latino Coalition was thrilled and the event was a smashing success. People came and mingled, ate and drank, and when the time came for the brief educational portion of the evening, Jess told the attendees about the Juneteenth beer and how she created it. The woman from the coalition then shared the history of Juneteenth and the audience asked questions and had a chance to talk and share.

Jess told me that working with the coalition on the Juneteenth event was a win-win for everyone: The woman from the coalition hosted the event in a cool brewery, generously offered at no charge.

The event attracted many people who had never stepped into Atrevida before and they fell in love with the brewery. Jess sold a lot of her special Juneteenth beer and, without having to "beat the diversity drum," it was clear to the audience that her business genuinely supports diversity in a very nondiverse community.

Then another interesting thing happened. Several weeks after the Juneteenth event, a business colleague of Jess called her and said she was trying to hire more diverse employees and did Jess have any idea where she could turn to find Black candidates? Yes! Jess immediately put her in touch with the woman from the coalition.

I told Jess that was a great story and she said, "The best part about it was meeting new people and working together on something. It was not only fun, but it also formed a bond and gives us all some equity in this relationship. Can you imagine if I hadn't participated and just called the woman from the coalition and said, 'Hey, do you have any Black people I can hire?' That would be totally uncool! But because we worked together, she knows me and *knows I want to help and she's happy to help me back.*"

That's a textbook example of the value of having business relationships with people who are different from you.

WHAT TO DO IF YOU DON'T KNOW ANY PEOPLE OF COLOR

If you know people of color, personally or professionally, share with them your goals for becoming a more diverse and equitable workplace and ask if they have any suggestions on diverse businesspeople you should meet and get to know or ways to become meaningfully involved in diverse communities.

But what if you don't know any people of color? You can still make inroads and build relationships that are mutually helpful and beneficial with diverse businesspeople, even without an introduction from a friend or colleague. Here are six ways to find and approach diverse businesspeople in your community:

1. **Identify local community resources that can help you directly or guide you to others.** Almost every community has a Chamber of Commerce, a YMCA or YWCA, an Out & Equal chapter

(a national nonprofit organization for LGBTQ workplace equality), or some similar organization. Many diverse communities also have a Black Chamber, Hispanic Chamber, Women's Chamber, Pan-Asian Chamber, and/or Native American Chamber, and in some communities, these different chambers have merged into one or formed alliances. Don't rule out churches and places of worship—their members are likely to be well-connected in the business community. A quick Google search can point you to numerous diverse organizations and the people who run them.

2. **Do your homework.** Dig into the diverse organizations you find online and identify which ones are doing work that you admire and that *align with your goals.* When you reach out to organizations, you'll want to be able to share *why* you would like to start a conversation with them. It will give you credibility with them. Keep in mind that diverse organizations are being bombarded with companies that want to partner with them. You want to stand out by offering specific ways you can help them achieve *their* goals, but you won't know what their goals are unless you dig in. Here's an example: AssetMark is a money management firm that works with independent financial advisors. Executives at AssetMark wanted to bolster the company's commitment to DE&I and wanted to make sure they "got it right." Esi Minta-Jacobs, vice president of human resources at AssetMark, said, "We want to make sure our contribution is impactful." They're using their expertise in money management to start a financial literacy program for underserved communities—what a great idea and a meaningful way to align what they do with creating long-term, positive change.

3. **Do not spread yourself too thin.** There may be so many options and worthy organizations that it can be overwhelming. It's better to start with one or two organizations that you feel you can really help than try to be involved with a dozen organizations and spread yourself too thin to do much good for anyone. Focus on no more than two groups so that you can make the greatest impact.

4. **Introduce yourself.** Get in touch with the organizations that you want to connect with and *start by genuinely complimenting them*

on their work in a particular area. Then share information about your company and your diversity efforts, and express interest in helping them with *their* objectives. Be honest and upfront about your goals and issues; truth breeds trust. Be sure to communicate how you want to help them. An email introducing yourself and your company or team could go like this:

> *My name is Steve Johnson and I am with the XYZ Company. The Black Latino Coalition of Colorado Springs is doing outstanding work with scholarship programs for local high school and community college students. At the XYZ Company, we believe that higher education should be accessible to all, especially underserved and diverse communities. We have created several programs of our own to help with this, but we feel that greater impact can be achieved if we work together with other community efforts. I'd like to have a conversation with you to learn how we can get involved in helping you achieve your goals, perhaps starting with support for your Spring Scholarship Donation Drive. I can be reached at 555-123-4567. Thank you.*

5. **Help before asking for help.** Have you ever had someone express interest in who you are or what you do, or offer to help you with something, but then learn that what they really want is for you to help them? It's the worst. You feel used. It's not just because their offer to help is insincere; it's also because it's opportunistic. And that's disrespectful. When working with other businesspeople and organizations, you must "pay your dues." When you sincerely help others accomplish *their* goals, you earn their trust and respect. That trust and respect earns you some equity and makes it OK for you to ask for help down the line. Jess at Atrevida demonstrated this: She helped the coalition host their event and even brewed a special beer just for them. Weeks later, when her colleague needed a connection, she knew she could provide that and that the coalition would be happy to help. You can't get without first giving.

6. **Show up.** Many community organizations are nonprofits, with limited budgets and finite resources. They depend heavily on volunteers to help get things done. Know this and offer your time (and your employees' time) to help with their efforts. Don't just write a check. Help them *do the work*. Your physical presence

counts. It also provides the opportunity to have genuine, meaningful, and ongoing conversations with people who may be different from you.

WHY CONTACT WITH PEOPLE WHO ARE DIFFERENT THAN YOU MATTERS

A few studies[1] suggest that diversity, equity, and inclusion training sessions don't really work to change employees' minds, attitudes, and behaviors. It's a discouraging thought. The studies reveal that there is a short-term uptick in working to eliminate bias or change behavior, but it doesn't last. To be fair, the studies show that the same pattern happens with almost *any* kind of training. For example, equipment safety training results in a short-term boost of safer work practices, but it doesn't last. That's why most types of training are ongoing: sales training, management training, leadership training, customer service training—you're never "done." Companies invest in ongoing training because stand-alone training doesn't change people. What does change people is *contact*.

Exposure to others results in real and lasting change. When we get to know someone and learn about them—their job, their family, their hopes and fears, their likes and dislikes, their sense of humor, their beliefs and values—we learn that we have more in common than we thought, that fundamentally, we're more alike than not. We learn that *people are people*.

The same studies that tell us that one-off diversity training doesn't result in lasting behavior change also tell us that contact with people who are different *does* result in lasting change. The conversations that you and your team have when working alongside people with diverse backgrounds *matter*. Show up. Listen. Talk. Share. And watch real change happen.

---

[1] David Brooks, "2020 Taught Us How to Fix This," *New York Times*, December 31, 2020, https://www.nytimes.com/2020/12/31/opinion/social-change-bias-training.html; Frank Dobbin and Alexandra Kalev, "Why Diversity Training Doesn't Work? The Challenge for Industry and Academia," *Anthropology Now*, 10, no. 2 (September 2018); Tiffany L. Green and Nao Hagiwara, "The Problem with Implicit Bias Training," *Scientific American*, August 28, 2020, https://www.scientificamerican.com/article/the-problem-with-implicit-bias-training.

CHAPTER 12
What to Do If You See or Hear Casual Racism or Sexism at Work

Over the course of your career, you've probably heard people at work say something that was racist, sexist, demeaning, or offensive, even if it wasn't directed at you. You may not have said anything or done anything about it, because, when it comes to work, it can be hard to speak up. Every company has its own culture and, in many organizations, the easiest thing to do is to let it go. After all, we're talking about *your job*. You have to work with these people, day in and day out. You think to yourself, "It's not smart to rock the boat. Just let it go." But it gnaws at you. Here's why "letting it go" is not the answer and why it makes you feel even worse:

- Those who make offensive, rude, and demeaning comments will continue to do so unless they are called out on it. They may not even know that what they're saying is wrong—or *why* it's wrong—but they sure won't understand that it's unacceptable if no one tells them.

- Offensive comments hurt and cause damage. For the target or recipient of the comment, they can be devastating. But others are also hurt by such comments. It's hard to hear a demeaning comment directed at someone you work with. And it's excruciatingly painful and awkward to witness someone being bullied or victimized by offensive comments. Even if you're just a bystander, not participating in the conversation at all, you can feel how awful and wrong it is, and it will affect you.

- If no one speaks up to confront a racist, sexist, homophobic, or xenophobic comment, onlookers will feel guilt. They know the offensive comment is wrong. They know someone should say something and stop it. If no one does, they will feel both *personal* and *collective* guilt. While these two kinds of guilt are different, the combination of them is highly destructive. Here is an explanation of each kind of guilt:

Personal guilt is on the individual bystander. It's the guilt a person feels because he or she did nothing in the moment to stop someone from harassing or attacking another. For many people, the reaction to witnessing another person being harassed is to freeze. Perhaps they don't know what to say or do or they just don't want to get involved, thinking, "This is none of my business." Or they're dumbstruck because they are so blindsided by hearing or seeing harassment that they can't fully absorb what is happening, let alone how they can help. They might fear confrontation or recrimination—or that *they* will become the next target. So they tell themselves, "This doesn't concern me" or "This isn't my battle to fight." But deep inside, they know they should have said something, yet they didn't. They may not be a bad person, but their inaction in the moment makes them feel like one. Their personal guilt becomes a weight on them and takes a toll with job stress, anxiety, and depression.

Collective guilt is different and, in my opinion, even more damaging. Collective guilt occurs when a group of people witness a verbal or physical attack on another, but no one in the group does anything to stop it. It's "collective" because the entire group is guilty of doing nothing. At work, if no one speaks up or does anything to help a coworker who is being harassed, there is a realization that "This is how it is here" or "Wow, this is who we are at this company." These are terrible concepts to absorb. It is hard to face—and accept—that you may end up saying to yourself, "Hurtful comments can be made at work, attacking a coworker, and no one will do anything about it, including me." This realization not only creates a sense of guilt in the bystander, but also shame. Shame is a huge and heavy burden. It doesn't go away easily or quickly. It can be so unbearable that people will leave an organization rather than feel ashamed of their company or how they, themselves, behave there.

COLLECTIVE GUILT IS CORROSIVE

My client Alison told me about a situation that created collective guilt. The organization she works for is a materials manufacturing company in the housing industry. It has always been a very male-dominated industry and has been slow to change as more women enter the field. Her company was doing a training series on its new products for twenty of its top customers. The attendees were all men, with the exception of one young woman, in her late twenties.

During the training session, the instructor was covering the mechanics of how a product functioned and said, "It's easy—anyone can do this, even 'little miss blondie over there,'" pointing to the young woman. There was a slight pause and then the people in the room, clearly uncomfortable with what had been said, chuckled a little bit. Some looked at the young woman to see her reaction; others looked down at the floor or just looked away. The young woman stoically carried on, but her face was bright red, either from embarrassment or anger. *No one said anything to the instructor.*

Alison learned of this incident after the fact and addressed it with the instructor, who said he was just trying to be funny and make a joke. He was written up and given a warning that if it happened again, he'd be terminated. But she told me that what surprised her most was that, over the next week, she received four emails from attendees who were at the training. She said that each of them, in their own way, expressed that they were horrified by what the instructor said to the young woman, that they felt terrible for her and how uncomfortable it was for them to witness the situation. They wanted Alison to know it happened and that it was wrong *and all of them said they regretted that they did not say something in the moment.* They were embarrassed that, in an entire room full of people, *no one* came to that woman's defense or said, "Hey, c'mon now, that's not funny." And they were embarrassed by their own lack of action in that regard. They didn't commit the offense, but they didn't speak up about it, either. They felt shame, enough shame that they took the time to write her an email.

I asked Alison if it made her feel a little better to know that these four men cared enough about the incident to follow up with an email like that. She replied, "Yes, I'm glad they emailed me. But I bet they'll never come to one of our training sessions again. They're too uncomfortable now." She is probably correct. Those four attendees are wrestling with both personal guilt and collective guilt. They don't want to face her.

You can see how destructive it can be to just be a bystander. From a business perspective, it can lead to employee (or customer) disengagement and a sense of futility: "Why try? That's just the way it is here."

Why wouldn't anyone in that training session speak up? Perhaps they simply didn't know what to say. But there is another possible reason: the bystander effect.

OVERCOMING THE BYSTANDER EFFECT

The *bystander effect* is a phenomenon that occurs when a group of people witness a problematic situation with another person, but no one will stop it or disrupt it. In fact, the greater the number of people who are present when "the problem" occurs, the less likely they are to intervene or help the person who is in distress. Why? It's the group dynamic: Being part of a crowd means that no specific person has to take responsibility for taking action. We can absolve ourselves: We may not have done anything to help, but hey, neither did anyone else.

To overcome the bystander effect, we must speak up when harmful, offensive, derogatory, or discriminatory things are said in our presence. To not do so is to be unintentionally complicit in the offense. You wouldn't be reading this book if you thought you were part of the problem. You want to be part of the solution.

Here are five tactics to combat casual racism or sexism at work, whether you're the target or a bystander:

1. **Use a comeback line to make your point.** Derald Wing Sue, a professor at Columbia who studies the psychology of racism, says that a comeback can be highly effective. "A person will say to me, 'You speak excellent English,' and I will say, 'You do, too,

John!'" said Dr. Sue, who is Chinese-American. The person giving Dr. Sue the "compliment" on his excellent English is also implying that he's an alien in his own country, not a true American. Dr. Sue states that "by simply reversing it, it can have a humorous or sarcastic impact" that showcases the intention of the comment and slaps it down.

2. **Be direct.** If you witness racism or sexism at work, you can speak up directly, right then and there. You can say, "Hey, knock it off" or "That's really out of line and not funny at all" or "Stop right there. It's not OK to say that" (or do that). Being direct does not mean you have to be aggressive, combative, or confrontational— it simply means that you are dealing with the situation directly, as it happens.

3. **Don't call them out; call them in.** Dr. Joy Pierce, a professor at the University of Utah, uses this technique often and says that it is highly effective and fosters constructive dialogue. She uses the example of a meeting in which an executive talked about *colored people*, a phrase that is very dated and associated with segregation and widespread discrimination of Blacks in the United States. Dr. Pierce states, "Rather than 'calling them out' on this offensive phrase, it's better to ask, 'When you say, "colored people," do you mean Blacks and African-Americans?' It's a straight-forward question, not an accusation. It also allows the person making the offensive comment to correct themselves, apologize, or clarify their comment. You'll get your point across and shine a light on what they said, but it also gives them the benefit of the doubt and the chance to better express *what they are trying to say.*"

4. **Check in on the person who is targeted, right then and there.** In the example I shared about my client's training session and the demeaning, sexist comment an instructor made in the class, a class attendee could have said, "Are you OK with that comment, Jennifer? Because I'm not. I think it's really offensive and disrespectful, to you and everyone else here." By checking in on the person who is targeted, you let them know that you stand with them in solidarity. You're also letting the person who made the inappropriate comment know that they are out of line and what they said won't be tolerated.

5. **Don't forget the saying "Better late than never."** When confronted with things that are overwhelming, uncomfortable, or frightening, people have one of three reactions: fight, flight, or freeze. At work, as a bystander witnessing a demeaning or racist comment being made to a coworker, "fight" would mean speaking up and defending your colleague and insisting that the perpetrator halt their insults immediately. "Flight" could mean leaving the meeting, leaving the conversation, or trying to change the subject. Flight is about avoiding confrontation altogether. It may be because you don't want to get involved. Or you don't want to become the next target. Or you're afraid that speaking up could hurt your career, especially if you're in a more junior role than the perpetrator. The third type of reaction, "freeze," is probably the most common. In the moment, you freeze because you simply don't know what to do or say. You're momentarily paralyzed and you do nothing. Perhaps your mind is racing with what you should say, or you feel completely trapped and overwhelmed in a terribly uncomfortable situation. You literally have no idea what to do, so you do nothing.

If you freeze in the moment, you may be flooded with guilt and remorse later. When your mind clears and your nerves calm down, you'll probably mentally replay the incident and think of all the things you could have or should have done. And you may feel just awful that, in the moment, your reaction was to do nothing at all. Your feelings can be worsened by the thought that "you missed the window" to say something and now the moment is gone. The good news is that the moment *isn't* gone. You can still speak up. And you can articulate your comments clearly, because you'll no longer be in "fight, flight, or freeze" mode. Gather your thoughts and follow up with both the perpetrator and the victim. A conversation with each might go something like this:

To the perpetrator:

Sarah, I want to speak with you because, in the meeting yesterday, you made a comment to Cliff that was really out of line. You said _____ and _____, and it was really hurtful, offensive, demeaning, and inappropriate. That's not who we are here at this company and it's not OK. I should have said something when it happened, but I was so stunned that my mind went blank. If it happens again, I will speak up, and I will report it to management.

To the victim:

Cliff, in the meeting yesterday, Sarah made a comment to you that was inappropriate, hurtful, and derogatory. When it happened, I was dumbstruck, and I didn't say anything. I want you to know that I am appalled that I didn't speak up at the time, but I have done so now. I talked to her and let her know it was unacceptable. I want to apologize to you, because I let you down in that meeting. I should have spoken up right then and there and I didn't. I'm sorry. It won't happen again. I also wanted to check in with you and see if you're OK and ask what I can do now. Please know that I support you, even if I blew it in the moment.

It is important to know that it's *never too late* to say something to both the perpetrator *and* your colleague. Not saying anything—ever—implies that there is general consensus that racist, sexist, or any offensive comments are OK.

In the next chapter, we'll tackle how to effectively recruit and interview diverse talent, including what *not* to say or do.

CHAPTER 13
Recruiting and Interviewing Diverse Candidates

You and your team have started talking, constructively, about race and diversity at work. You're following the STARTING Method and you're reaching out to various business organizations in your community and online to help spread the word about employment opportunities at your company. Great job! But before you actively start to recruit and interview diverse candidates, there is some work you have to tackle internally first. You must eliminate inherent bias in your process and prep your team for their role in diversity hiring.

HOW TO STOP "PICTURING" YOUR IDEAL CANDIDATE AND ESTABLISH OBJECTIVE CRITERIA

In Chapter 2, you learned that we all have bias, that even babies have bias! When it comes to work, bias can be in our minds (what we picture when we think of the "right" candidate) or it can be embedded in the recruiting process at your company, through job descriptions or a bonus program for employees who refer others to the company. Bias that exists in our minds can be discussed and dissected to break it down. It's important to do this, because if you or your team have a picture in your mind of the kind of person you want to hire, it can be very difficult to change that mental image.

For example, if you want to hire a truck driver, perhaps you picture a man in his forties who has more than twenty years of trucking experience. So if a woman in her late twenties applies or shows up for an interview, would you consider her for the job or rule her out? What about names? One study showed that "Jamal" needed eight more years of experience than "Greg" to be seen as equally qualified. Résumés of men with elite backgrounds were called back for interviews *twelve times* more often than identical résumés of men with non-elite backgrounds.

That kind of bias is hard to work around—*unless* you've discussed it with your team first and have identified the *skills* and specific qualifications you're looking for in a candidate. Make sure everyone is objectively focused on *what's required for a position*. For example, PNC Bank listed *qualities* that would make a new team member successful. Its list includes *self-disciplined, patient, customer-focused, proactive in managing risk*, and *independent*. If you identify specific skills and qualities for positions and evaluate candidates on those criteria, rather than on whether they match "who you pictured," you'll be headed in the right direction.

HOW TO REWRITE JOB DESCRIPTIONS TO REMOVE BIAS

Review your job descriptions. It's likely that your job descriptions have bias embedded in them, although that may not have been the company's intention. There are words and phrases that promote gender, religious, race, generational/age, and ability bias. If you create more inclusive job descriptions, you will capture a more diverse pool of candidates. Here are some examples of gender bias phrases:

- Female-focused words:

  agree, empathetic, sensitive, support, collaborate, trust, interpersonal, nurture, understand, compassion, share
- Male-focused words:

  aggressive, confident, fearless, ambitious, dominant, strong, assertive, independent, decisive, outspoken, driven, challenge, pressure

Another interesting finding in diversity research is that women will typically apply for a position only if they *meet 100 percent of the requirements*, whereas men "go for it", even if they don't have all the required experience. You certainly don't want to deter women from applying for your jobs, so examine your job descriptions to see if there are any requirements that are nonessential and remove those. You can clearly indicate the required skills and qualifications and then list "preferred" skills. By doing this, you won't discourage women candidates who have the essential skills, but may need training in other areas that are nonessential, from applying.

How to Write More Inclusive Job Descriptions

- Never mention race, ethnicity, gender, or age. It's illegal.
- Avoid phrases like *clean-shaven* that would exclude candidates whose faith requires them to maintain facial hair (this phrase also suggests that the position is for men only).
- Avoid *native English speaker*, since people can be fluent in a language without being "native" to a particular country. Instead, use *fluent English* or *proficient English*.
- Avoid *legal citizens only* or *illegal*, as in *No illegals may apply*. Instead, use *No undocumented immigrants or refugees may apply* or *Must be authorized to work in this country*.
- Avoid *recent college grad* or *young*. Instead, use *entry-level opportunity*.
- Avoid *must have 3–5 years of experience* and use instead *must have a minimum of 3 years of experience* (this phrasing would not exclude someone who has more experience).
- Avoid *must be able-bodied* or *must be strong* and replace with specific requirements for a position—for example, *This role requires moving equipment that weighs up to 50 lb.*
- Use *Latinx* instead of *Latino* or *Latina*, which refer to Hispanic men or Hispanic women, respectively.
- Avoid *maternity/paternity leave* when covering leave policies. Use *parental leave* instead, which is more inclusive because it includes adoptive parents, surrogate parents, and same-sex parents.
- Avoid using *he/she* and instead use *they/them*, *people*, or *the candidate*.
- Avoid job titles that are gender slanted, such as *waitress* or *salesman*. Use instead *server*, *waitstaff*, or *sales representative*.
- Avoid words and phrases that connote a young age or youth-oriented culture, such as *work hard*, *play hard*, *digital native*, *party atmosphere*, or *young and energetic*. It's OK to use phrases like *fast-paced* or *deadline-driven* to communicate that business moves

quickly, but you don't want to exclude an older candidate from applying.

- Avoid words such as *rockstar*, *ninja*, and *superhero*, which are words that are associated with men and may deter women candidates from applying.
- Avoid *cultural fit*. Instead, use *value alignment*.
- Avoid *must have own car*. Instead, use *must have access to reliable transportation* where applicable.

HOW TO FIND DIVERSE TALENT

After you've reviewed and rewritten your job descriptions to make them more inclusive, it's time to get the word out and reach as many people as possible with the news that your company has jobs! Your objective now is to "put the welcome mat out" for diverse talent and attract them to your company, team, or department. Where do you start?

- First, don't keep your search for diverse talent a secret. Tell *everyone*! Start with your own employees and ask them to help spread the word. Tell vendors and suppliers, clients and customers, and your social circle (neighbors, friends, and acquaintances). You never know who might know someone you should interview.
- If you already have diverse team members at your company, ask them if they'll share and promote your job openings to their networks. Ask the same of your Employee Resource Groups. You'll usually find that diverse employees are more than happy to help spread the word about job openings; they serve as important "ambassadors" who can speak to your company's commitment to diversity.
- Use LinkedIn. It can be a gold mine for recruiting. You can connect to specific groups on LinkedIn and post job openings, share company updates, and search for qualified candidates. You can also "reverse engineer" your search, meaning that, instead of searching for diverse candidates, you review your own diverse employees' profiles and explore their educational, professional, and LinkedIn

groups. You can then join those groups and post your job openings within those groups. LinkedIn has a "Diversity Hiring Playbook" (see Appendix).

- Post your job openings on one of the sites listed on "Best Job Boards for Diversity and Inclusion" (see Appendix). You can drill down to numerous sites that have specific job boards for companies looking for military and veterans, Indigenous people, people of color, women, LGBTQ+, retirees and older workers, workers who are age 50+, those with disabilities, students, people from other countries, and neurodiversity (people of specific developmental, intellectual, or cognitive abilities, such as those with autism or who are on the spectrum).

- Post your goal to create a diverse and inclusive workplace on your website, either on the homepage or on dedicated tabs for "Diversity" and "Job Opportunities." It's OK if you have the message in more than one place on your website. When people are considering changing jobs, they're taking a chance on a new workplace dynamic, so let them know upfront that you are actively seeking to diversify your workforce. I've seen some great corporate websites where the *main message* on the company's homepage is their commitment to diversity. Don't bury the message. Make it prominent.

- Find organizations that serve diverse communities and ask to meet with them. Introduce your company and let them know that you have professional opportunities and that you're looking for terrific people who can help represent the diverse community you serve. If you don't have any diverse employees, let them know that. Say, "We aren't a very diverse organization, and we know we need to change that. We're trying to meet with different local community groups to get the word out about the opportunities we have at our company. I'd like to talk with you about what we do and the kinds of jobs we have. I'm hoping you can share the information and help us get the word out." Even if you have diverse employees, you'll want to continue to attract new and diverse talent, and you can apply this approach. In my experience, you'll be welcomed with open arms, because everyone understands the value of good jobs and most organizations are happy to help support local job growth.

- Universities, colleges, community colleges, and vocational schools are great places to spread the word about your jobs and commitment to diversity. Most have regular job fairs and expos near the end of the semester. Contact the schools and learn how you can share your job opportunities with their student bodies. Don't rule out high schools. If you have entry-level jobs that don't require experience and you're willing to train, high schools would love to hear from you. That's because there is increasing pressure on teachers and schools to help students find jobs when they graduate. When a high school student graduates, they typically take one of three paths: They go on to college or community college, they join the armed forces, or they go to work. Why not have them work for you? A large commercial insulation company finds their diverse employees this way. They stress "no experience necessary" and "all training provided" and they have filled their open positions with diverse, young talent straight out of high school. Not only have they become a very diverse company, they also have stopped the "brain drain" that was occurring at their company. Their older workers were retiring, and they desperately needed to attract new people to their company. Working with local high schools solved the problem.

HOW TO INTERVIEW DIVERSE CANDIDATES

To effectively evaluate diverse candidates, it's critical to prepare your team and teach them some new approaches for interviewing. Here are best practices for interviewing that have been shown to yield strong results for recruiting diverse talent:

- Limit your employee referral pool. Many businesses rely on their employees referring people they know to apply for jobs. This is often a great approach. However, the problem is that your employees likely know people who are a lot like they are and that can create a very homogeneous group of candidates. It may seem like a contradiction: Employee referrals can be the best kind of referrals, but they often perpetuate a very nondiverse team. If you're interviewing candidates who were referred by employees, make sure you limit the number and balance it with an equal or greater number of candidates who come to you through different channels.

- Insist on a diverse candidate pool. Insist on accountability. In Chapter 7, I shared the goals that Levi Strauss & Co. set for itself on diversity, and one of those goals was to have half of all candidates for open positions be from diverse or minority groups.

- Use a diverse set of interviewers, whether it's people of different experience levels, genders, ages, races, ethnicities, or backgrounds. Their various perspectives can be highly valuable. Additionally, *Forbes*[1] states that women on an interview panel are a strong magnet for women candidates. Women are more likely to join a company when they can interact with women who are already there. In fact, recruiting experts say that one of the biggest deciding factors in whether or not a woman accepts a job offer is if there was a woman on the interview panel. *A diverse panel will hire a diverse workforce.*

- Ask each candidate *the same, skills-based questions*. This allows you to fairly evaluate responses against the same criteria.

- Don't waiver from the required qualifications for a select few candidates that you "like." When interviewing, *stay true to the qualifications and skills you've identified that candidates must have.* If you don't, your process will not be fair and equitable.

- Keep in mind that lived experience is not a replacement for professional expertise. Don't hire the wrong person for the job simply because they "check the diversity box" for a certain group. That's the worst kind of tokenism and it hurts the hired employee, the rest of your team, and your company's reputation. Hire the professional expertise you need, with the goal of *also* hiring diverse talent.

- Emphasize your company's commitment to diversity, equity, and inclusion and support that with examples of projects, practices, and community involvement to make it real.

---

[1] Maynard Webb, "How to Alter Your Hiring Practices to Increase Diversity," *Forbes*, October 29, 2017, https://www.forbes.com/sites/maynardwebb/2017/10/29/how-to-alter-your-hiring-practices-to-increase-diversity.

These steps will help you find, attract, recruit, and hire new and diverse talent. In the next chapter, you'll learn how to strengthen your talent (and your organization) with effective networking, mentoring, professional development, and job promotions.

CHAPTER 14

Mentoring, Networking, and Checking In: Three Big Ways You Can Help Your Diverse Employees Succeed

Chapter 13 covered recruiting and interviewing people of color and other minority groups. Let's assume that you've been successful in making good hires with new and diverse talent. Congrats! Now you need to make sure that your hires *succeed*. Although you hired people who are qualified and bring diverse perspectives to the table, you can't just throw them into your team, department, or organization and expect them to flourish. They're going to need your support and backing if they are to *fulfill their potential*.

Even if your organization doesn't have formal programs in place to support diverse employees, there are three key ways you can help ensure their success: mentoring, networking, and checking in.

MENTORING

Have you ever had a really great boss or supervisor? If you're lucky enough to say "yes," think back to what made them so great. Aside from their own talent and experience, I'm betting that what made them "great" was that *they supported you*. Whether it was spending time with you, teaching you and providing insights, giving you new challenges, or introducing you to new people and opportunities, your great boss *invested in you and had your back*.

When people feel supported, their confidence—and accomplishments—grow. Employees who feel supported are not afraid to ask questions or seek clarification or direction on a project. They're more likely to reach for new heights because they know their bosses won't let them get in over their heads. They strive to do more and be more, because the support they receive underscores that *they are not alone*. They have the tools to do their jobs and the support they need to keep advancing.

I was lucky to have a great boss when I was in my early thirties: Pete Rentschler. I was working for Nissan's global ad agency. The automotive industry was (and still is) very male-dominated and this was no different at the ad agency handling the Nissan account. I worked exclusively with men: from the dealers, to the Nissan team, to my own team. There were seven regional offices, each with their own staff, budgets, and business strategies. Pete promoted me to run the Dallas office. Overnight, I inherited a five-state territory and had twenty-three employees. It was a *huge* step up for me, and I had never faced a challenge like this before. I had kicked butt in my previous role, but this was different: I suddenly had more than twenty people in four departments to manage, I had almost 200 Nissan dealers to keep motivated and informed on all marketing initiatives, and I had a Nissan Regional client to partner with to create effective marketing campaigns. Oh—and I was also the first woman to ever be in this role. My six counterparts were all men, as were all of my clients and dealers.

The spotlight was on me and I felt the heat of it. I felt the pressure to succeed, so that other women in the company would know that they, too, could succeed and be promoted. I felt the pressure to be as good as my male counterparts, even though they'd been in their positions for years (or decades) and I was a newly promoted rookie. I felt the pressure to run a profitable regional office with little or no turnover, even though I'd never run an office before. It was exciting, nerve-racking, and totally overwhelming.

As nervous and intimidated as I was, I was never scared, because *Pete had my back*. Without making a big deal out of it, he made sure I was supported in this new role. He and I had weekly meetings and daily phone calls to discuss specific work projects and to just to talk about how things were going for me. In those conversations, he imparted lessons, advice, and insight. And he served as a sounding board for me, a trusted ear and "safe space" for me to discuss the daily challenges I faced. Looking back on it, I know now that he mentored me and made sure I got the professional development I needed to succeed. But at the time, it mostly felt like I had a great boss who believed in me and who wanted to show the rest of our large organization *why I was the one he had chosen*.

Pete never coddled me. It was quite the opposite: he pushed me—and he pushed me *hard*. He gave me "stretch" assignments that were incredibly challenging for me, but that made me grow professionally in big ways. There were times I loved him and times I loathed him, but I always knew that he'd never give me more than I could handle. He would not let me fail. He was a profound influence in shaping my career in the years to come. But make no mistake: I was not Pete's pet project. I was *part of his job*. His job was to put the right people in the right positions across the company and help them succeed in those positions. *My success became his success.*

As a leader, your job is to make sure your team members have what they need to succeed. Beyond overseeing their work and performance, *your job is to get them ready for the next opportunity in your organization.* With any employee, the time you spend to professionally grow and develop them is important, to their success and yours.

With diverse employees, it's *imperative* that you set them up to succeed. Why? Why should diverse employees receive more support from you or your organization? Why should extra steps be taken to ensure their success? Isn't that playing favorites? Or worse, pandering? Nope.

Mentoring and developing diverse team members is fair for four reasons:

1. Many minority employees do not see themselves reflected in leadership roles within organizations. It's difficult to make serious inroads in management when none of the company leaders are from a minority group. Diverse employees may not have a sense of what it takes to rise to that position because they don't see anyone like themselves in those positions. Additionally, while White men tend to identify mentors on their own, women and minorities more often need help in finding a mentor. Connecting employees to mentors can help close the gap and provide the support needed to succeed within your organization.

2. Research shows that both women and minorities are more susceptible to self-doubt and the "imposter syndrome," which is when an individual has serious doubts about their abilities and

qualifications, despite evidence to the contrary. An ongoing mentoring or professional development program can build confidence, as well as skills.

3. Mentoring and developing talent helps address the "first rung" problem. Many companies today seek to hire diverse C-suite-level or leadership executives and complain they can't find many qualified candidates at that level. But the culprit actually resides at the bottom of the "ladder of success." Workplace and employment studies have found that getting to the "first rung" in job advancement is the most important step. If an entry-level or junior employee does not get promoted to the very first career rung, they fall further and further behind. *The more they fall behind, the harder it is to catch up.* It's like learning to read. If you or anyone you know struggled to learn to read as a child, you know that if reading isn't mastered by about age 7 or 8, everything after that becomes harder and harder. Learning becomes impaired. If you fall behind in reading at that age, it is very, very difficult to catch up. The key to having more qualified diverse talent at the *top* is to start at the *bottom*, making sure that employees get to that important "first rung."

4. Supporting your diverse employees is the *very definition of inclusion*. Minority groups have long been excluded from many professional roles and organizations. Therefore, they may lack the professional network of peers in a given industry, simply because there are no peers. For example, the oil and gas industry is a very homogeneous, overwhelmingly White and male industry. A woman or person of color in that industry would likely feel very isolated and alone, with no one to talk to and share experiences with. Mentoring and development sends a message of "We see you, we want you here, and we support you."

When mentors teach their protégés the ropes and endorse them for additional training and high-visibility assignments, they give them the breaks they need to develop and advance. Those who have mentors say it's "very important" and essential to their professional growth. Mentors are guides, coaches, and sounding boards. Even if your company or organization doesn't have a formal mentoring program, you can still be a mentor to someone, like my boss Pete was to me. Mentors are also often connected to people who can really help move an employee's career forward, which leads me to the importance of networking.

NETWORKING

I mentioned Dr. Joy Pierce in an earlier chapter and she shared with me a story about her own experience as a mid-level executive in climbing the ladder early in her career. Joy is Black and her boss was White. One day, her boss called her to her office and told her a VP in the company would be retiring in six months. She asked Joy if she would be interested in the position. Joy leapt at the opportunity and said, "Yes!" Her boss then said, "Ok, there are several committees you need to be part of to learn about this position. It will be important for you to fully understand the position so that when the time comes, you're ready. I can get you on those committees and make sure you have the visibility and connections you'll need to position yourself for the job." Wow! Her boss *opened big doors* for her! Much of business revolves around connections, referrals, and who you know. Many people get jobs because of someone they know in an organization or industry. Networking and expanding one's professional visibility are *incredibly important*. But diverse employees may lack the kind of networks that help them professionally. They may not play golf and know the guys at the country club that perhaps you know. They may not have wide networks of people who are leaders in their communities who can vouch for them or endorse them. They may not have gone to an Ivy League school that makes their résumés stand out. They may not even know many people in their organizations who are at higher levels than they are.

Aside from being connected to people who can help someone get ahead professionally, networking offers another benefit: advocacy. In many organizations, the decisions about who can and should fill an open position take place in meetings, hallway interactions, and informal conversations.

Imagine this scenario: A meeting is being held to discuss an upcoming open position of Supervisor. The conversation goes like this:

Top executive:	"Who do we think is best for this position?"
Executive #1:	"Robert Smith would be great. I know him well. We play golf together occasionally and he's terrific."
Mentor/advocate:	"Ramon Diaz would be great. I've been working with him for the last six months and he'd be perfect for the position."
Top executive:	"Ramon Diaz? Haven't heard of him. Who is he?"
Mentor/advocate:	"He's been in Warehouse Operations for two years now and he's crushing it. He implemented a system that saves 15 percent on shipments and cut delivery times by a third. He's got the respect of the entire team and knows how to get things done. He has the skills we need for this position. I highly recommend you take a look at him and talk to him."

In this example, you can see how important an advocate can be. Conversations about jobs and people happen all the time, in all kinds of circumstances. An effective network can also be effective advocacy. You can help your diverse team members by advocating for them for the right professional opportunities.

CHECKING IN

You can also help your employees by doing regular check-ins with them, asking them how things are going, if there is anything they need, or if there is anything you can help with. This keeps the line of communication open and creates ways for *both* of you to talk about little things that can come up in day-to-day business. Not every issue or situation that comes up at work needs a big meeting. Sometimes a casual conversation works better. By doing regular check-ins, you create the moments in which conversations can be candid and less structured than a meeting. This is a good thing to do with *all* employees, not just diverse employees. Some of the best business insights and opportunities that might not have come up in a formal meeting are brought up in informal conversations.

The next four chapters cover important areas that leaders need to address to make real and lasting progress on diversity, equity, and inclusion.

PART IV

Lead Your Colleagues, Customers, Partners, and Employees

CHAPTER 15
The Leader's Role: Guiding and Setting the Example

There is a great deal of talk about the need to make companies and organizations more diverse, equitable, and inclusive. And that's good. But we have to move from talking about diversity to *doing* something about it.

IF YOU'RE A WHITE MALE IN A LEADERSHIP ROLE, YOU CAN CREATE CHANGE MORE THAN ANYONE AND MORE THAN YOU REALIZE.

If you are a White male in a high-level position, you might be one of the few people who can really create change. That's because several studies and surveys show that nearly half of Black employees feel it's *never* acceptable to discuss their experiences with race and bias,[1] and Black professionals who aspire to senior leadership positions avoid discussing race altogether, for fear that it will hurt their chances of advancement.

Other research[2] shows that women and other minorities are often scrutinized and criticized for supporting diversity in a way that White men are not. One study showed that when women and other minorities engage in behaviors that demonstrate that they value diversity (respecting cultural, religious, gender, and race differences; working with diverse team members; and managing people from different racial or cultural backgrounds), it made no impact on how their bosses rated their performance or competence. In fact, those who were rated as *frequently* demonstrating diversity-valuing behaviors were rated much *worse* by their bosses! When White men engaged in

---

[1]Laura Morgan Roberts and Anthony J. Mayo, "Toward a Racially Just Workplace," *Harvard Business Review*, November 14, 2019, https://hbr.org/2019/11/toward-a-racially-just-workplace.

[2]Stefanie K. Johnson and David R. Hekman, "Women and Minorities Are Penalized for Promoting Diversity," *Harvard Business Review*, March 23, 2016, https://hbr.org/2016/03/women-and-minorities-are-penalized-for-promoting-diversity.

those same behaviors, they did not get rewarded with a higher score for their performance, but they did not get dinged either. The conclusion of the study was that, while White men do not get rewarded for demonstrating that they value diversity, women and non-Whites actually get punished for it.

The bottom line for White men in leadership positions is this: *You can champion diversity in a way that will be seen and heard as credible*. Because you're White, you're not viewed as someone who may be intertwining a business initiative with personal life experience. You're uniquely positioned to talk about diversity and move it forward within your organization.

If you're *not* a White male and you're in leadership, this doesn't necessarily mean you're going to face resistance, but you do have to be smart and careful about it. I speak at approximately eighty conferences a year on the topic of diversity and why it's so important for business, and a comment I hear a lot from audience members is this: "It was so refreshing to hear you talk about diversity without 'waving a flag.' You don't have an agenda. I am tired of people trying to shove their views down my throat."

Now, let's dissect what's going on in a statement like that. What the person is really saying is that, because I'm White, my words and thoughts on this topic are perceived to be "neutral"—that I'm not preaching diversity because I have an axe to grind. It's unfortunate that people of color aren't afforded the same assumption. Apparently, when people of color discuss the importance of diversity, it can be perceived as an issue that is important to them (and only them), stemming from personal grievance.

If you're a leader and a woman or a person of color, I believe the best way to counter that perception is to *frame diversity as a business opportunity*. Chapter 4 covered the merits of diversity, equity, and inclusion extensively. By stating the business case for diversity and framing it as "this is critical to our growth and profit," you take yourself and your personal experiences out of the equation. Sure, some people will wonder if you're championing diversity because of who you are. But if you stick to the *irrefutable metrics* that have shown that diversity is highly beneficial to business, you won't come across as "waving a flag." Imagine if you were having conversations about technology advancements or social media platforms as a way to communicate with customers. No one would think that you support those business issues because they're personal. You'd make the case for why your company needs to adopt certain methods and approaches and those recommendations would be supported by data and performance metrics. Take the same approach with diversity. Be neutral and discuss the facts, the opportunity, and the business case for diversity.

If someone asks if you are coming at this from a point of personal experience, you can answer truthfully and say, for example, "As a Black person (or any member of a diverse group) *of course* I have my own life experiences with racism and diversity, and I am happy to share those experiences with the team if that would be helpful. But this discussion and my recommendations are not coming from a selfish view of what I want or what I think is right. We must approach this the same way that other leaders are, in other companies and industries. The business case for diversity is strong and irrefutable, and for this reason, it should be viewed as an important and valid growth strategy, not a social justice or humanitarian exercise."

IT'S TIME TO WALK THE TALK AND LEAD BY EXAMPLE

Every leader has heard it: "Lead by example." Every newly promoted manager or supervisor is given this advice. Even people who aren't in formal leadership positions know that "lead by example" is one of the best ways to build a strong team, foster trust, and move business forward. It's good advice, because in business, people are always watching you. Your employees watch everything you do, because you set the tone and the standards for your company, your team, your brand, or your department. Customers watch you, too. They want to know if the things you do align with the words you say. Leading by example is a way of doing business. It's never about cutting corners or compromising your corporate or personal values. Leaders must consistently demonstrate commitment to their corporate beliefs and goals through actions, day in and day out.

That's why companies that say they value diversity, but don't back that up with any meaningful, tangible examples or efforts, don't come across as credible. Audi learned this the hard way when it ran its "Daughters" commercial during the Super Bowl. The ad featured a father and his young daughter, with the father thinking to himself, "Do I tell her that despite her education, her drive, her skills, her intelligence, she will automatically be valued as less than every man she ever meets?" It was intended to show support for gender equality and, specifically, equal pay for equal work, but it backfired right away. At the time the ad aired, Audi had *no women* on its executive team and the percentage of women on its supervisory board (the German equivalent to a U.S. board of directors) was far below the average percentage of Fortune 500 firms. Audi was skewered on social media and business websites for the apparent hypocrisy and the ad on YouTube has garnered twice as many "dislikes" as "likes." *Credibility comes from actions, not words.* Your efforts to make your work environment more diverse and inclusive must be sincere, or they will fall flat. And everyone watching will see.

Good leaders walk the talk. When it comes to making your company or team more diverse, equitable, and inclusive, it's imperative that you back up your words and intentions with actions. As a leader, you must be able to address the elephant of race and inequality in the room. The elephant is there, taking up a lot of space, and it's not helpful or constructive if everyone is trying to maneuver around the elephant while pretending it's just not there. The elephant is in the way! It's blocking your team's ability to get to what's next. This is your chance to lead by example. If your team sees that you can handle a sensitive or tough conversation, that you're not shying away from it, and in fact, you're modeling how to have productive dialogue about it, they learn that they can handle the same. You can teach them how to discuss the issues of race, diversity, equity, fairness, and inclusion at work, as well as all the feelings and questions associated with these. You do this by fostering safe discussion about topics that were previously off the table or deemed way too touchy to tackle. I wish I didn't have to write this next part, but it's important.

HOW TO GUIDE YOUR EMPLOYEES WHEN HORRIBLE, RACIST THINGS HAPPEN IN THE WORLD

When you were a child, you were taught "how to be." Someone taught you right from wrong, how to say, "I'm sorry," how to treat others fairly and respectfully, how to study and learn. As a child, you had a *lot* of questions. You asked your mom or dad, your relative or guardian, your teacher or neighbor, or religious leader your questions, and they guided you. At times, you had questions that may have made them uncomfortable or were difficult to answer—perhaps questions about death, divorce, pain, fairness, love, jealousy, teamwork, abandonment, responsibility, or honesty.

I am betting that, no matter how difficult the questions were, the person or people who guided you did their best to give you *truthful* answers, even if their answer was "I don't know." I'd also bet that many of your questions or discussions about those important topics were complex and layered, requiring multiple conversations over years. Whoever was helping you and teaching you "how to be" was there for you, and they were patient with your questions and the many twists and turns that weighty conversations can take. They guided you through life's complicated and difficult layers and helped set you up to succeed as a person.

The truth is that horrible, racist things will happen. People will be attacked because they're "other." These atrocities have happened in the past and they will happen again. A mass shooting. A bombing. A riot. A beating. A noose. When horrific events happen, we have a reaction—and a need to talk about them. Your employees may think they can't, or shouldn't, discuss these things at work. But when people are traumatized by horrific events, they can't just go about their jobs, business as usual. They are distracted, their hearts ache, and they can't focus. The only thing that can help is to talk about it and share how they feel. As a leader, *you can guide them through this and have a productive conversation that leads to action.* You can't do anything about horrible, violent acts in the world. But you can use those awful moments to let your team express their feelings and discuss what you and your team *can* do to make your workplace and your community better. Here are do's and don'ts that can help when something horrific happens:

DO address the event. Perhaps it's something in the news, such as a racially motivated death or an attack on a synagogue or mosque. Perhaps you've identified a problem within your organization that you need to rectify. Use this moment to reiterate your company's values and let your team know that you take a stand against racism and inequity at work.

DO say something. Believing that societal problems outside of work don't affect your people is not wise. Your employees need clear communication about what you, as an organization, do and don't support. Do you support the need for change? Do you believe DE&I is a priority and that it's worth the investment and effort required to make it concrete? Saying nothing at all is the *opposite* of good leadership.

DO consider the emotional toll and acknowledge how hard this is on everyone. Horrific events leave scars on your workers, especially Black and other minority employees. Allow your employees to express their emotions. They may feel anger, fear, confusion, and turmoil. They may even be disengaged from work, which psychologists say is a sign of trauma.

DON'T gloss over traumatic events, believing that discussing them reopens the wound. Don't communicate "Let's buck up and get through this." If you prioritize productivity over your employees' natural reactions to traumatic events, you will come across as oblivious, clueless, and heartless.

DO allow for discussion among team members. Your employees are not robots. They need to process their own feelings as well as those of their teammates. They may want to talk to each other as a group or one-on-one. Give them time and space for conversation. That's how support groups function: They are effective because people share their feelings with others who listen and share. Healing and hope are found when people have time to pause and share their feelings.

DON'T expect all of your employees of color to be comfortable discussing race at work. Don't ask them to explain racism or share their thoughts unless they volunteered to do so on their own. Don't put them on the spot and ask them to speak "from their experience."

DO use this moment to identify a way that your company or team can support diverse communities beyond your workplace. Employees value the internal support and efforts you make to create a more diverse, equitable, and inclusive environment at work. But you can underscore your commitment by taking actions within your community to make a difference. It could be offering a scholarship contribution to a student from a diverse high school or community college. Or creating internships for young people who aspire to work in your industry. Or working with a local mentoring program and allowing team members to mentor others on company time. People feel *hopeful* when they can do something to help.

DON'T use community actions and support to draw attention away from the internal challenges you have at work. Nothing will come across as more insincere, inauthentic, and pandering than supporting your diverse community or giving attention to racial or social inequality *outside* of work when you are ignoring the issues *inside* that need to be resolved.

Kwame Christian is an author, mediator, and speaker who spent years at the Kirwan Institute for the Study of Race and Ethnicity. Now, as the director of the American Negotiation Institute, he says that difficult conversations are important to have—because they're happening anyway. He states, "My motto is: The best things in life are on the other side of a difficult conversation." I agree. Just because a conversation or topic is uncomfortable and stressful doesn't mean we should avoid it. In fact, the only way to feel better (and in business, do better and be better) is to tackle those conversations head on.

The American rock band O.A.R. has a song titled, "I Go Through." It's a song about how hard it is to have difficult conversations. My favorite lyrics are from the chorus: "You go 'round and around it. You go over and under. I go through."

Good leaders lead by example. They go *through*.

In the next chapter, we'll tackle the extremely touchy area of tokenism, why it's so destructive to an organization, and how to avoid it.

CHAPTER 16
Reducing Tokenism and Bias: Give Your Diverse Employees and Suppliers a Genuine Seat at the Table

I once read something about gaining and losing weight that struck me with its simplicity and wisdom: "Gaining weight is unintentional and easy. Losing weight is *intentional* and *difficult*." I read it years ago, but it has always stayed with me. While preparing for and then writing this book, I kept thinking that companies that are diverse—or those that are not—could be described the same way: Becoming a nondiverse company is *unintentional* and *easy*. Becoming a diverse company is *intentional* and *difficult*. I don't believe that most all-White companies set out to be nondiverse; they didn't *intend* for it to happen—they just evolved into it. It's *easy* to fall into hiring the same types of employees who have always worked well in a corporate culture, who "fit a mold." And the companies that work to make their organizations diverse and equitable and inclusive? They work with *intention*. They plan, create strategies, learn, and evolve, and they work their butts off.

I think it's an important distinction, because I have talked to some executives and leaders who feel that "demographics are our destiny" and that they don't really have to "do" anything to drive diversity efforts. They believe that the changing demographics of the United States and the world will just "naturally" bring them more diverse talent over time. I don't think that's a safe assumption. I believe that what will happen is that terrific, qualified, diverse people will be drawn to the *best* companies, not just *any* company. Candidates who are high-potential, who can move business forward, and who can make an impact are the candidates *everyone* will want, and those candidates will be drawn to companies that make diversity an *intentional* priority. It's not realistic to expect that the best talent will just come to you by default.

With so much emphasis on diversity, equity, and inclusion in the workplace, companies are eager to hire diverse employees. That's a good thing if the intention is to create a better, stronger, more successful company. But in many cases, it seems that the intention is to get a badge of honor—"LOOK HOW DIVERSE WE ARE!!!"—rather than truly delivering on the promise of diversity and what it can do for business. It smacks of tokenism.

The *Oxford English Dictionary* defines *tokenism* as "the practice of making only a perfunctory or symbolic effort to do a particular thing, especially by recruiting a small number of people from under-represented groups in order to give the appearance of sexual or racial equality within a workforce." I don't think most of us need a formal definition of *tokenism* though; we know it when we see it. It's awkward because it comes across as so fake, insincere, and *so, so obvious,* like "Excuse me, your strategy is showing."

What can you do to make sure your desire to create a diverse workforce doesn't lure you into the trap of tokenism? The following section offers key do's and don'ts to avoid tokenism.

AVOIDING TOKENISM IN HIRING

1. **DO** recognize that diversity, equity, and inclusion are a *journey,* not a checklist of the right numbers. If you hire new people from diverse groups, but they have no real role in helping your company become more equitable and inclusive, all you've accomplished is, well, adding some new people. If you think of diversity as a *policy transition,* it will lead to broader opportunities and multiple ways to create a truly diverse workforce. Instead of asking, "Where can we find a Black candidate, an Asian candidate, a disabled candidate, and someone who is LGBTQ+?" ask instead, "How can we make our jobs more visible to a diverse candidate pool? And how can we make both our jobs and our company interesting, appealing, and promising to diverse candidates?"

2. **DON'T** hire diverse talent and not give them a voice in helping shape your company culture. All that does is reinforce "checklist culture" and the sense among other workers that diverse employees were hired because they were the right gender, race, religion, age, etc.

3. **DON'T** turn your diverse employees, or suppliers, into your "diversity flag." What I mean by that is that many companies want to showcase their diversity, so they put a diverse employee or rainbow flag in their marketing messages. It comes down to intention: If you're featuring diverse employees in group photos on your website or making sure they're at local community events to show everyone how diverse you are, you'd better back it up with their real contributions and involvement. Tonja is a Black businesswoman. She created a natural, healing herb paste that helps with pain management and has numerous other health benefits. It's been selling well, particularly in the Black community. After the death of George Floyd, a large, multistate grocery chain approached her, wanting to carry her product in their stores. Sounds good, right? But wait for it . . . Tonja requested (several times) a meeting to discuss the sales plan, including the cities and number of stores the product would be in, as well as their forecasts and goals, so she could make sure her production and supply were adequate. The grocery chain team told her, "You don't have to worry about that; it'll be fine." One executive told her that she should "just be happy that you're at the table." Two things then happened: First, the grocery chain placed an order of 70 units. Yep, just 70. Those 70 flew off the shelves in a day and the chain ordered more. Then more. Then even more. Then even *more*. When more than 1,300 units had been sold, in just a few days, the chain then asked for photos of Tonja so they could feature her on their website. Tonja said, "They never took me seriously. I wanted a *sales meeting* and they said no. But they sure wanted my headshot up on their site to show how diverse they are."

4. **DO** represent your *real* diversity status on your site or in marketing messages (don't show groups of diverse people if you only have one or two), and make diversity relevant to what your associates do or how your company works. Let's say you have a Hispanic woman, Sofia, and an Asian man, Yuki, in your organization, and they work in the Sales Department and in Customer Service, respectively. Featuring them on your website in those relevant areas about your company would be appropriate. So would featuring them under "Our Commitment to Diversity," as long as the verbiage highlights their contribution to diversity (beyond their race). For example, "Sofia joined the company two years ago and

has helped grow sales in new markets throughout the Southeast. She also mentors young women locally and serves as the treasurer for the Hispanic Women's Chamber of Commerce." Or "Yuki's prior role in creating exceptional customer experiences in the hospitality industry has brought a new level of customer care to our company. Yuki is also an accomplished chef and teaches a weekly Asian-fusion culinary class at Harris Community College."

5. **DON'T** assume that it's "one size fits all" when it comes to your company's employee accommodations and benefits. This is an area that many companies overlook when making diverse hires. When everyone is pretty much alike (for example, White and Christian), it's easy to build a company culture and work patterns that work for everyone, such as designating Christmas Day and Good Friday as company holidays. But what about the needs of employees who come from other cultures? If your company is committed to making diversity and inclusion really work, you may need to rethink things to which you've never given a second thought. What about people with various health issues or abilities? And those with different family structures, which can affect their parenting hours? What about people who need a different schedule of holidays? I have worked with Muslim and Jewish coworkers who sighed and rolled their eyes at the utter lack of regard given for *their* religion's holy days. One way that companies can address the myriad of diverse accommodations is by offering a broader spectrum of "choose your own benefits," where employees can choose those that matter to them most and fit their lives and lifestyles best. For example, a small business can offer employees a set number of personal days that can be used to observe any holiday or take time off for any reason. The goal is to make employment work for everyone.

AVOIDING TOKENISM IN DEVELOPMENT AND PROMOTIONS

Almost everyone knows someone who shouldn't have been promoted to a job or role they weren't ready for. It happens a lot, because people often get promoted for reasons that have little or nothing to do with the way they do their job. Maybe their manager likes them. Or they've "been at the company forever." Or "it's time to have a person in that role who is a woman/Black/Hispanic/Millennial/Gen Z/openly gay or lesbian or trans/disabled/veteran." You want your employees to succeed. And you want your diverse talent to rise through the ranks and become leaders at your company. But you *don't* want anyone to say that an employee was promoted because of their diverse or minority status or that they didn't earn the promotion. It must be made clear to your entire team that professional development and promotions are fair and equitable.

In Chapter 14, we covered a leader's role in mentoring and professionally developing diverse talent. The bottom line is that a leader's job is to prepare employees for advancement. Getting them ready for a new role or responsibilities is part of *your job*. But we know that unconscious bias affects our judgment and decision-making, and when it comes to promoting someone, that's what you have to watch out for if you want to be a truly fair and equitable organization.

When you've groomed, developed, and prepared your diverse employees for the next role in their careers, how can you make sure they get a fair shake and are considered on their qualifications and merits, not the color of their skin or their age or who they know? Here are two key steps to take that will bolster equity and fairness in promotions:

1. From the outset, be *clear and transparent* about how training, promotions, and pay decisions are made. If there are guidelines or "rules" for paygrades and titles, and minimum qualifications required for specific positions, publish those internally and then *stick to them*. Nothing smacks of tokenism more than a diverse employee (or *any* employee) who gets a promotion without earning it. Equity is about creating a fair and level playing field for all. Think about sports and how referees make calls. They don't play favorites. They stick to the rules of the game and all the players know what the rules are and agree to play by those rules.

2. Create a fair process. According to an article in the *Harvard Business Review*,[1] a law firm accomplished this with a five-step system:

---

[1] Joan C. Williams and Sky Mihaylo, "How the Best Bosses Interrupt Bias on Their Teams," *Harvard Business Review*, November/December 2019, https://hbr.org/2019/11/how-the-best-bosses-interrupt-bias-on-their-teams.

- Step 1: Start with a specific outline of the responsibilities and expectations of a particular role and what is needed for someone to advance to that role.
- Step 2: Identify every employee who meets the requirements or shows tremendous potential, and create an *anonymous list of eligible candidates* (Employee A, Employee B, etc.).
- Step 3: Assign the anonymous employee candidates to one of three groups: GREEN (those who meet the specific job requirements), YELLOW (those who are close to meeting the requirements, but do not) or RED (those who do not meet the requirements).
- Step 4: Provide the color-coded, anonymous list to the evaluation team—the decision-makers. Because the data is anonymous and the candidates are already grouped by qualifications and competencies, favoritism is eliminated, and no employee candidate is overlooked.
- Step 5: Require evaluators to adhere to the predetermined benchmarks, ensuring that *the best candidate* is identified and promoted.

Sidenote: The law firm that created this system provided employees who were placed in the yellow category with training and advice about how to move up to the green level. They were told, "You're not quite ready for this promotion now, but you're close. We want to make sure you have the opportunity to go for it in the future and here's what you need to work on. We'll help by providing the additional training that will get you ready." Fantastic! That demonstrates a true commitment to equity.

I love this example because it's simple, no-cost, doable, and *fair*. It requires no third-party consulting, just time spent upfront to establish clear "rules" and a transparent process. It's the complete opposite of tokenism. Hiring or promoting someone solely because they help you "check the diversity box" is the worst. Don't do it. Resist attempts to be pushed in that direction.

The next chapter tackles how to deal with naysayers and derailers, two challenging personality types that you are bound to come across in your organization.

CHAPTER 17
Dealing with Naysayers and Derailers

My friend Robin works at a mid-sized accounting firm. Accounting is one of those industries that is overwhelmingly White. The owner of the firm is trying to diversify their staff because he knows their team will be strengthened if they have new talent with new perspectives. Many of the clients they serve are small to mid-sized businesses and the business owners themselves are more diverse than ever.

Aside from being an all-White firm right now, the staff at the accounting firm is comprised of a lot of older accountants who think diversity is a "bunch of nonsense" or "just caving in to political correctness." Robin said to me, "The owner of the firm is trying to do the right thing and make change at our firm, but it's like pushing the elephant up the stairs. A lot of the team doesn't take any of it seriously or thinks it's all just B.S. and I don't know if we'll be able to do this if the team isn't on board and supportive."

This is a common issue many leaders face when working to create a workplace that is more diverse, equitable, and inclusive. Their all-White or mostly White team thinks it's unnecessary, stupid, or a waste of time. Change at work is always hard for most employees because it requires new approaches and relearning or training, and *most employees like things just the way they are.*

When it comes to putting the work in to make your team, department, or company more diverse, you should expect some resistance from your team—maybe not from all of them, but there are almost always a few who "like things just the way they are." They don't want to change, and they don't want to have to filter their comments (because they know that they often say things that are either overtly or mildly racist or inappropriate). They don't want to sit through any diversity training. They think DE&I is just a new "business trend" that companies are doing to make themselves look good.

As a leader, you need to be alert to this mindset within your team, and you need to address it *head on*. You cannot be wishy-washy on this matter. You cannot start this effort and then abandon it. You can't let those who aren't supportive of this (at least in their actions at work) drive your business. *You're* the driver. You set the direction and you take the wheel. Naysayers and derailers will sabotage your efforts and prevent your success if you don't confront their objections and destructive actions and nip them in the bud. Let's talk about what kinds of comments and behavior you can expect to deal with.

NAYSAYERS

Naysayers fall into two groups: Those who start trashing an effort before it's *even begun* and those who find fault in everything *along the way*. Naysayers do nothing to help solve problems or address issues that inevitably come up. Naysayers will make comments that consistently belittle an initiative or put down the people doing the real work. Here are examples of the types of comments that naysayers make:

- "I've been here for twenty years. I've seen this kind of thing come and go. This won't last. It's the 'flavor of the month' approach."
- "This will never work. A friend of mine works for a company that tried this, and it was a huge failure."
- "Ha—let's see how THIS goes! No one asked US what we thought of this." (Note: This kind of comment can lead to sabotaged efforts because the naysayer feels overlooked and wants to prove that without them or their input, nothing will work.)

Naysayers are toxic to your organization, especially when it comes to creating a more inclusive workplace. To truly build an inclusive culture, you need people *pulling together* to make things happen, not poking holes in new ideas and saying, "It'll never work." On top of that, their chronic complaining slows progress and hurts morale.

Here are three ways to deal with naysayers and get them to shift from negative, unhelpful comments to positive, constructive input:

1. **Create a time and place for input and ideas.** This is important, because naysayers often do their damage *after* a meeting or

behind your back. While some naysayers are bold and challenge everything, others are quite insecure and petty and will only disparage ideas and efforts when "the coast is clear." By creating specific times for discussion and ideation, such as regular meetings, you also create the appropriate environment where criticism and concern can be brought up for discussion. If the naysayer is trashing efforts behind the scenes, you can call them on it and say, "Ed, in our weekly meetings, you haven't shared your concerns about this, but I've heard that you feel we're making a big mistake. The purpose of these meetings is to collectively discuss our progress. If you have something to say, this is the place to do so. It's inappropriate to do otherwise." (*Side note:* I read an article once about a study that found that the word *inappropriate* is highly effective. No one wants to be inappropriate, especially at work. The study said that even small children understand that being "inappropriate" is not OK. It stated that children respond better and behave better when told, "Stop that—it's inappropriate" versus "Stop that—that's very bad." It's a powerful word. Use it when you must keep someone in line.)

2. **Use optimism.** Naysayers tend to be pessimistic. They see the flaws in everything instead of seeing the possibilities. They focus on problems instead of solutions. By using optimism to direct the conversation, they won't have a platform for their negative comments. Optimism forces people to focus on what *can be done*, rather than what *can't*. Here are examples of how to use optimism to shift a naysayer's focus to find productive outcomes:

   - "Ed, let's talk about what's working so far before we get into the problem areas."
   - "Ed, what suggestions do you have for improvement?"
   - "Ed, what would you like to see changed for the better?"
   - "Let's take the position that we're going to be successful with this. What do you suggest we do next to ensure we're on track for success?"

3. **Confront naysayers about the destructive comments they make.** Confronting naysayers shines a spotlight on their duplicity (saying one thing, or nothing, in a meeting, then saying something critical later). "Ed, in our meeting last week to finalize our out-

reach programs for diverse candidates, you expressed no concerns, and, in fact, you nodded agreement with our approach. I've learned that you actually feel the approach is flawed and you have questions about things that we'd already reached agreement on last week. I was surprised to learn this so late in the process. You're withholding your opinions when we can discuss them together and solve problems, then later you're saying you've had concerns all along. That's unacceptable. It wastes everyone's time and doesn't move us forward. You need to be a productive member of the team, *contributing appropriately*." This is a warning shot. Once you've addressed this and told the naysayer to contribute appropriately, you're in position to use stronger language if it happens again: "Ed, we talked about this. This cannot and will not be tolerated. It stops right now. Do you understand? If it happens again, your job is at risk." Or "If it happens again, we'll need to make some changes. It's up to you, Ed."

These three tactics should be used in the order above. The first one sets the stage for constructive collaboration. If that doesn't work, the use of optimism and focusing on what will work creates a framework that doesn't enable the naysayer's chronic complaining. Finally, confronting the naysayer lets them know they're out of line and that there are consequences.

DERAILERS

Another challenging type of employee is the derailer. Unlike a naysayer, a derailer might not be negative or pessimistic at all. They can be outwardly positive, masquerading as a "team player," while actually sabotaging your progress in passive and insidious ways. Derailers can be dangerous to your efforts, and they can be hard to spot. Here are seven behaviors that will help you identify potential derailers within your team:

- **Selfish.** They are not a team player.
- **Disengaged.** They do just enough to get by. I call them *coasters*. They just coast along on the work of others.

- **Untrustworthy.** They fail to keep their word or commitments. Other team members do not trust them. They will share information that was told to them in confidence.

- **Emotionally reactive and unpredictable.** They're impatient or a hothead, or both, and are prone to exploding at others, so people try to avoid working with them.

- **Unfair.** They play favorites, blame others for their own mistakes, or put disproportionate work on some while giving others easy assignments.

- **Closed-minded.** They're unwilling to try new ideas, listen to feedback, or explore others' views.

- **Info-hoarding.** They withhold information. They don't share important information or updates with others, thereby ensuring that team members or projects fail.

As a leader, it's imperative that you identify naysayers and derailers and work to change them. You must be direct with them, outlining their behavior and why it's unacceptable. You must make it clear that *change is necessary* if they want to keep working in your organization. You'll help them by guiding them and providing feedback on their progress, but it's *up to them to get on board*.

It's not easy. But your success with DE&I depends on building a culture that everyone understands, accepts, and participates in. One of my clients, Toyota, has a saying: "You can change the people. Or you can change the people." Toyota gives their associates every opportunity to improve and succeed. They coach them and, if necessary, provide additional training. They actively work to change and better their employees if they are not performing their jobs well. But ultimately, if they are unable to change the people, *they change the people*.

CHAPTER 18
You're Not Finished. Keep Trying. Keep Evolving.

This is the last chapter of this book. You've invested time in reading it. Even before you started reading it, I know you devoted time and reflection to the topic of race at work. You now have a specific method and tools for creating—or continuing—your diversity, equity, and inclusion efforts at your company or within your team. This book has covered a lot of do's and don'ts. I want to provide you, a leader, someone with influence and position, a few more that will be very important to your ongoing success with DE&I.

DON'T "launch and abandon." One of the worst things a company can do is to make a big deal about a new initiative or program, and then over time, it sputters out and fades away. It happens often at large companies. Not only does it leave employees confused and bewildered, but it makes them *jaded*. They can become so accustomed to "launch and abandon" that they don't take anything seriously and, therefore, they don't invest themselves fully. Creating a successful DE&I plan and keeping it moving forward is not like other aspects of your business. It's more personal and human. Most people don't have "feelings" about a sales plan or a production plan. But diversity, equity, and inclusion are *people-centric values*. If your efforts in this area are minimized over time or abandoned completely, it's a slap in the face to all of your employees. This is about *them*. Guard against "launch and abandon." It will be difficult to recover momentum and restart a plan if your team is skeptical and disengaged.

DO assess progress. In the STARTING Method, the "G" is for goals. Keep track of your progress on your goals, and if you find that progress is slowing or stalled, identify why. Address the problems that impede your progress or hold your team back. If your team sees that progress on achieving goals is consistently assessed, it drives home that this is an important company initiative that is *here to stay*.

DON'T be afraid to refine your plans along the way. This is a *journey*, not a *task*. In Chapter 10, I said the STARTING Method was named that because your DE&I efforts will never be "finished."

You'll garner new insights and learn new approaches. You'll talk with other leaders and learn best practices. Your employees will inspire new ideas and suggest refinements and changes. Modifying your approach throughout the journey sends a strong message to your team that you are committed to making this really work.

DO expect to educate. And repeat. And repeat. . . . You'll get questions and feedback, including resistance or pushback from employees on this journey. Your job is to continuously remind and reinforce why DE&I is important and the proven benefits of this effort and investment. Don't deviate from the business case for diversity.

DO keep your ear to the ground. Listen to the "hallway" chatter to learn if your team is struggling with aspects of your DE&I efforts. Good leaders are not afraid of the problems they know about. They are afraid of the ones they *don't* know about. Encourage questions and comments and provide forums for hearing those and addressing them. A good leader does not shy away from questions from their team, even uncomfortable questions. A good leader welcomes questions because in the question lies the concern, confusion, fear, resentment, stubbornness, hope, or anxiety that the questioner is feeling. It's the "real real," showing itself in the form of a question. Keep your finger on the pulse of what's going on and expect your managers and department heads to do the same.

DO celebrate success. On March 28, 2019, I was giving a keynote speech for an internal meeting at GE Appliances. I will never forget that day, because at the beginning of the program, Rick Hasselbeck, the chief commercial officer, made a big announcement: GE Appliances had just been notified that they earned a *perfect score* for the Human Rights Campaign's Corporate Equality Index (CEI) for the *third year in a row*. When Hasselbeck made the announcement, the room *erupted*. More than 300 employees were attending the meeting and they went *wild* with joy! They cheered, shouted, fist-bumped, danced, and hugged each other. Some even cried with joy. I had never seen anything like it. They were so excited and thrilled, because this perfect score reflected *their work*—their efforts, their commitment, and their dedication. Being recognized by the highest organization in the United States with a perfect score for their DE&I efforts was like winning the Super Bowl. This award was theirs. They earned it. Celebrate the successes of your team and their accomplishments. Celebrate progress and wins, big and small. If your team solves a challenging problem, celebrate it. If they open the door to a new relationship with a diverse business or community, celebrate it. If they meet or exceed the goals you've established, celebrate. Honor them with recognition and celebration for their hard work and their successes. It will come back to you tenfold.

DO set new goals and strategies to strengthen your ongoing efforts. Your DE&I journey will likely have some interesting twists and turns along the way. You don't know what you'll encounter or where this path will take you. Be open to the opportunities that present themselves, and continually set new goals and create new strategies that keep your efforts moving forward. When you achieve an established goal, celebrate! And then set a *new goal*. Treat this as you would any other aspect of your business and continually press forward, asking, "What can we do next?"

Talking about race isn't easy. It shouldn't be easy. It's complex, emotional, challenging, and *human*. We were never taught how to do this. It requires bravery. But good leaders do brave things all the time. They look the tough stuff in the eye and then they get to work to tackle it.

Thank you for reading this book. In the second chapter, I told you that you're a good person. I'll end the same way. I am honored that you, a good person, spent time to learn how to do better and be better. You're equipped now to make a difference, with your team, with your company, in your community, and in society. Lead by example. And know this: *Your efforts matter.*

APPENDIX
Helpful Terms and Resources

HELPFUL TERMS

BIPOC: *Black, Indigenous,* and *people of color.*

DE&I: *Diversity, equity, and inclusion.*

From the Ford Foundation (https://www.fordfoundation.org/about/people/diversity-equity-and-inclusion/):

- *Diversity:* Diversity is the representation of all our varied identities and differences (race, ethnicity, gender, disability, sexual orientation, gender identity, national origin, tribe, caste, socioeconomic status, thinking and communication styles, etc.), collectively and as individuals.
- *Equity:* Equity seeks to ensure fair treatment, equality of opportunity, and fairness in access to information and resources for all.
- *Inclusion:* Inclusion builds a culture of belonging by actively inviting the contribution and participation of all people.

From the University of Michigan (https://diversity.umich.edu/about/defining-dei/):

- *Diversity* is where everyone is invited to the party.
- *Equity* means that everyone gets to contribute to the playlist.
- *Inclusion* means that everyone has the opportunity to dance.

LGBTQ+:

Lesbian, gay, bisexual, transgender, queer (or sometimes *questioning*), *and others*. The "plus" sign represents all other gender identities and sexual orientations, including pansexual and two-spirit. (*Two-spirit* refers to a person who identifies as having both a masculine and a feminine spirit and is used by some Indigenous people to describe their sexual, gender, and/or spiritual identity.)

POC: *People of color.*

Structural Racism:

From the Aspen Institute (https://www.aspeninstitute.org/blog-posts/structural-racism-definition/):

- *Structural racism* is a system in which public policies, institutional practices, cultural representations, and other norms work in various, often reinforcing ways to perpetuate racial group inequity. It identifies dimensions of our history and culture that have allowed privileges associated with "whiteness" and disadvantages associated with "color" to endure and adapt over time. Structural racism is not something that a few people or institutions choose to practice. Instead it has been a feature of the social, economic, and political systems in which we all exist.

From the Catalyst website (https://www.catalyst.org/research/structural-racism-black-americans/):

- *Structural racism* is a long history of discriminatory and dehumanizing laws and policies that have created and exacerbated inequality in almost every sphere of life. These laws and policies are built into the fundamental structures of our societies—our systems of labor, housing, education, voting, healthcare, and justice. An overarching system of racial bias across institutions and society that gives privileges to White people resulting in disadvantages to people of color.

Systemic Racism:

From the U.S. Equal Employment Opportunity Commission (EEOC) (https://www.eeoc.gov/advancing-opportunity-review-systemic-program-us-equal-employment-opportunity-commission):

- Examples of systemic practices include: discriminatory barriers in recruitment and hiring; discriminatorily restricted access to management trainee programs and to high-level jobs; exclusion of qualified women from traditionally male-dominated fields of work; disability discrimination such as unlawful pre-employment inquiries; age discrimination in reductions in force and retirement benefits; compliance with customer preferences that result in discriminatory placement or assignments.

White Privilege:

From Merriam-Webster (https://www.merriam-webster.com/diction-ary/white%20privilege):

- The set of social and economic advantages that White people have by virtue of their race in a culture characterized by racial inequality.

HELPFUL RESOURCES

Best Job Boards for Diversity and Inclusion

https://diversity.social/diversity-inclusion-job-boards/#gsc.tab=0

Energetic Awakenings

www.energeticawakenings.com

David Phillips is the founder and president of Energetic Awakenings in Cleveland, Ohio. He is a workshop leader and group facilitator for many organizations dealing with the challenging topics of racism, conflict, and LGBTQ+ cultural competency.

Harvard Business Review's 10 Must-Reads on Diversity

https://store.hbr.org/product/hbr-s-10-must-reads-on-diversity-with-bonus-article-making-differences-matter-a-new-paradigm-for-managing-diversity-by-david-a-thomas-and-robin-j-ely/10275

LinkedIn Diversity Recruiting Guide

https://business.linkedin.com/talent-solutions/c/13/10/the-diversity-hiring-playbook

Index

A

AbeTech, 105
Accents, 70
Acceptance, 55, 94
Accommodations, employee, 164
Accounting industry, 169
Acknowledgment, 74, 92–93
Action, importance of, 55, 61, 119–120
Adversarial versus dis-content, 72
Advocacy, 143–144
Aging skier problem, 23, 24–25
Alison's story, 121–122
Angie's story, 80
Apologizing, 74

Arguing, listening without, 95
Asian applicants, 93
Asking questions, 74, 95–96
Aspen Institute, 182
AssetMark, 112
Atrevida Beer Co., 109–111, 113
Audi commercial, 151–152
Awkwardness, acknowledging, 67

B

Babies:
  bias in, 15–16
  having, 43
Benefits, employee, 164
Berardinelli, Tatiana, 58, 62
Bergh, Chip, 60–61, 102–104

Bias:
  babies and, 15–16
  blind spots from, 17
  in business, 17
  in decision-making, 17
  defined, 15
  denial of, 18–19
  in disagreements, 17
  harmful effects of, 17
  in hiring, 17
  implicit, 16, 17
  in job descriptions, 130–132
  opportunities missed as
    result of, 27
  recognizing, 16, 129–130
  unconscious, 16, 17
BIPOC, as term, 181
  See also Blacks; People of color
Black Latino Leadership
  Coalition of Colorado
  Springs, 110–111
Blacks:
  candidates, 39–40, 93
  car doors locking around, 59
  demographics, 27
  employees, 68–69, 149
  fears, 58–60, 68–69, 149
  journalists, 39
  skiers, 23–24
  See also People of color
Blame, avoiding, 98
Blind spots, 17
Bootstrapping argument, 82–84
Boundaries, respecting,
  68–69, 98–99
Business, effects of bias in, 17
Business case for diversity,
  31–35, 150–151
Butler-Morton, LaTreece, 58–59
Bystander effect, overcoming,
  122–125

C
Candidates:
  Asian, 93
  Black, 39–40, 93
  diverse, 129–136
  qualified, 39–40, 79–81
Car doors locking around
  Blacks, 59
Catalyst website, 182–183
Checking in, 123, 125, 144–145
"Checklist culture," 162
Childbearing, 43
Christian, Kwame, 155
Christmas, 49, 56–57
Closed-mindedness, 173
Coasters, 172
Collective guilt, 120–122
Colleges, 134
Color-blindness, 47–48
"Colored people," as term, 123
Comeback lines, 122–123
Comments:
  confronting naysayers about
    destructive, 171–172
  made by employees resistant to
    change, 79–84
  offensive, 47–50, 119–125,
    171–172
  positive, 50
  racist, made by employees
    outside of work, 84–86
  by Whites, 47–50
Common ground,
  finding, 67–68
Community colleges, 134
Community resources, 111–112,
  133, 154–155
Competitive "edge," 32
Competitors, 42
Compliance versus
  acceptance, 55

Conflict, handling, 71–73
Confronting naysayers, 171–172
Consistency, lack of, 54
Contributions, validating, 96–97
Conversations, one-on-one, 56–57
Corporate Equality Index, 178
Creary, Stephanie, 67
Credibility, 152
"Culture fit," 42
Customer comfort/attitudes, 41–42
Customer service, 32

D
"Daughters" commercial, 151–152
Debating versus discussing, 72–73
Decision-making, 17, 32, 33–34
Defensiveness, 16, 72, 95
DE&I (diversity, equity, and inclusion) efforts:
  failure of, 53–55
  as intentional and difficult, 161
  results, sharing, 60–62
  as term, 181–182
  training, 114
Demographics:
  aging population, 23, 24–25
  racial/ethnic, 23–24, 27
Derailers, dealing with, 169–170, 172–173
Development, avoiding tokenism in, 164–166
Dignity, 98
Directness, 123
Disagreements, 17, 80

Discussing versus debating, 72–73
Disengagement, 172
Diverse candidates, 129–136
  bias, recognizing, 129–130
  criteria, objective, 129–130
  finding, 132–134
  interviewing, 134–135
  job descriptions and, 130–132
Diversity:
  business case for, 31–35, 150–151
  decision-making and, 32, 34
  defined, 181, 182
  excuses for avoiding doing anything about, 39–43
  investment in, 43
  as policy transition, 162
  as political hot potato, 5–6
  in skiing, lack of, 23–24, 25–26
  as term, 54
  White reluctance to talk about, 5
Diversity, equity, and inclusion (DE&I) efforts:
  failure of, 53–55
  as intentional and difficult, 161
  results, sharing, 60–62
  as term, 181–182
  training, 114
"Diversity flag," 163
Diversity of thought, 105
Downhill skiing:
  aging skier problem, 23, 24–25
  diversity, lack of, 23–24, 25–26

E
Edible Arrangements, 65
Educating others, 178

Ellis, Eric, 55
Emotional reactiveness, 173
Employee accommodations and
    benefits, 164
Employee referral pool,
    134–135
Employees:
  diverse, 69–70
  gay, 99
  racist events, guiding employ-
    ees after, 152–155
  racist or toxic, 42
  resistant to change, 79–84
Energetic Awakenings,
    183–184
English language proficiency,
    70, 122–123
Equal Employment Opportunity
    Commission, 183
Equality, 83–84
Equity, 83–84, 182
Example, leading by, 151–152
Excuses, 39–43
Experiences, personal, 58, 73, 96
Expressing oneself, safety for,
    94

F
Facts, overlooking/ignoring,
    33–34
Fair treatment, 48
Fears, 58–60, 68–69, 149
Fierro, Jess, 109–111, 113
Fierro, Rich, 109–110
"Fight, flight, or freeze" mode,
    124
First Amendment, 85
"First day on the job" conver-
    sations, 96
"First rung" problem, 142

Floyd, George, 7–8, 55, 110, 163
Forbes, 53–54, 135
Ford Foundation, 181–182
Forward movement, 69
Freedom of speech, 85
Friction, handling, 71–73

G
Gay employees, 99
GE Appliances, 178
Gender bias phrases, 130
Goals, 101–105, 177, 179
Golden State Foods, 65, 67–68
Groupthink, 33–34
Guilt, collective versus
    personal, 120–122

H
Hanukkah, 49, 56–57
Hart, Kevin, 23–24
Harvard Business Review,
    165–166, 184
Hasselbeck, Rick, 178
HBCUs (Historically Black
    Colleges and Universities), 40
Heim, Chris, 105
Helping before asking
    for help, 113
High schools, 40
Hiring:
  bias in, 17
  excuses for lack of diver-
    sity in, 39–43
  objective criteria in, 129–130
  post-hoc justification in, 18–19
  "quality" in, 40
  tokenism, avoiding, 162–164
Hispanic/Latinx population, 27
Historically Black Colleges and
    Universities (HBCUs), 40

Honesty, 55
Human Rights Campaign's
    Corporate Equality Index,
    178
Human value, basic, 94–95

I
"I Go Through" (O.A.R.), 155
"I'm not racist or biased," 48–49
Implementation, poor, 53
Implicit bias, 16, 17
Imposter syndrome, 141–142
Inclusion, defined, 182
Inconsistency, 54
Info-hoarding, 173
Input, creating time and place
    for, 170–171
Interest, expressing sincere, 68
Interrupting, listening
    without, 95
Interviews, 134–135
Investment, 43, 100
"Invisible race," 67
Irick, Jaime, 55, 58, 61–62
"I treat everyone the same," 48

J
Jack's story, 82–83
Jewish traditions, 49, 56–57
Job boards, 183
Job descriptions, 130–132
Jonah's story, 97
Journalists, Black, 39
Juneteenth, 103, 110–111
Justification, post-hoc, 18–19

K
Katz, Rob, 25–26
Kendi, Ibram X., 49
Ku Klux Klan radio station,
    48–49

L
Language proficiency,
    70, 122–123
Latinx, as term, 131
Latinx/Hispanic population, 27
"Launch and abandon," 177
Leadership:
    buy-in and support by, 54
    diverse, 32
    leading by example, 151–152
    people of color in, 150–151
    racist events, guiding employ-
        ees after, 152–155
    White men in, 149–150
    women in, 43, 150–151
Learning, 69, 73, 74, 89–90
Levi Strauss & Co., 60–61,
    102–104, 135
Levi Strauss Foundation, 103, 104
LGBTQ+, as term, 182
LinkedIn, 132–133, 184
Listening, 68, 72, 95, 178

M
Marketing, representing real
    diversity status in, 163–164
Mboun, Cheik, 65
Meetings, discussing rac-
    ism in, 57–58
Mentoring, 139–143
Minta-Jacobs, Esa, 112
Mistakes, recovering after, 74
Moving forward, 69

N
Names:
    changing, 6, 70
    discrimination based on,
        92–93, 129
    mocking, 71
    repeating/learning, 70–71

National Association of Black
  Journalists, 39
Naysayers, dealing
  with, 169–172
Networks and networking,
  40–41, 105, 143–144
Nissan's global ad
  agency, 140–141
Nurturing talent, 100–101

O
O.A.R. (band), 155
One-on-one conversa-
  tions, 56–57
Optimism, 171
Orange Grove Consulting, 42
Organizations, professional, 105
Outcomes, focusing on, 98

P
Page, John, 65, 66, 68
Pause button, pushing, 73
"People not like you,"
  as term, 54
People of color (POC):
  finding and approach-
    ing, 111–114
  as individuals, 99, 154
  as leaders, 150–151
  as term, 182
  treatment of, 55–56
  See also Blacks
Personal experiences, 58, 73, 96
Personal guilt, 120
Perspectives, different, 23, 26–27
Pessimism, 171
Phillips, David, 184
Pierce, Joy, 123, 143
Plans, refining, 177–178
PNC Bank, 130

POC (people of color):
  finding and approaching,
    111–114
  as individuals, 99, 154
  as leaders, 150–151
  as term, 182
  treatment of, 55–56
  See also Blacks
Policy transition, diver-
  sity as, 162
Political hot potato, diversity as,
  5–6
Post-hoc justification, 18–19
Poverty, 82
PPG (company), 55, 58, 62
Predictability, lack of, 173
Privilege, White, 66–67,
  82–83, 183
Problem-solving, 69
Professional organiza-
  tions, diverse,
  105
Progress on goals, assessing, 177
Promotions, 41, 99, 164–166

Q
Qualified candidates,
  39–40, 79–81
"Quality" in hiring, 40
Questions:
  asking, 74, 95–96
  by employees resistant
    to change,
    79–84

R
Race, talking about:
  awkwardness,
    acknowledging, 67
  boundaries, respecting, 68–69

common ground,
  finding, 67–68
debate, avoiding, 72–73
defensiveness, avoiding, 72
do's and don'ts, 69–71
experiences,
  acknowledging, 73
forward movement, 69
friction/conflict, handling,
  71–73
importance of, 65–66
interest, expressing sincere,
  68
learning, being open to, 73
listening, 68, 72
in meetings, 57–58
in one-on-one conversa-
  tions, 56–57
pause button, pushing, 73
problem-solving, focus on,
  69
recovering after mistakes, 74
sincerity, 66, 68
small, starting, 67–69
White privilege, acknowl-
  edging, 66–67
White reluctance for,
  66–67
Racism:
  denial of, 81
  learning about, 69
  structural, 182–183
  systemic, 183
  as term, 55, 61
Racism at work, 119–125
  action, importance
    of, 119–120
  bystander effect, overcom-
    ing, 122–125
  collective guilt, 120–122

personal guilt, 120
Racist, as term, 48–49
Racist comments made by
  employees outside of
  work, 84–86
Racist employees, 42
Racist events, guiding employees
  after, 152–155
Ramírez, Liliana, 67
Randy's story, 59–60
Recovering after mistakes,
  74
Recruiting diverse talent,
  132–134
Reframing conflict, 72
Relationships, building,
  109–114
Rentschler, Pete, 140–141
Resistance, 53
Resources, helpful, 183–184
Respect, 58, 94–99
Résumé, "Whitening", 93
Robin's story, 169

S
Samantha's story, 80
Selfishness, 172
Sexism at work, 119–125
  action, importance
    of, 119–120
  bystander effect, overcoming,
    122–125
  collective guilt, 120–122
  personal guilt, 120
Shame, 120, 121
Showing up, 113–114
SHRM (Society for Human
  Resource Management),
  54
Sincerity, 66, 68, 90–91

Skiing:
    aging skier problem, 23, 24–25
    diversity, lack of,
        23–24, 25–26
Small, starting, 67–69
Snowboarding, 24–25
Society for Human Resource
    Management (SHRM), 54
STARTING Method, 90–105
    acknowledgment, 92–93
    goals, 101–105
    investment, 100
    nurturing talent, 100–101
    respect, 94–99
    sincerity, 90–91
    tools, 99–100
    transparency, 91–92
Structural racism, 182–183
Success, celebrating, 178–179
Sue, Derald Wing, 122–123
Systemic racism, 183

T
Talent, nurturing, 100–101
Talking less, listening more,
    68
Tasha's story, 96
Teasing, avoiding, 97
"Those people," as term, 71
Thought, diversity of, 105
Tokenism, 161–166
    about, 161–162
    defined, 162
    in development and promo-
        tions, avoiding, 164–166
    in hiring, avoiding,
        162–164
Tonja's story, 163
Tools, 99–100
Toxic employees, 42

Toyota, 173
Transparency, 91–92, 165
Trustworthiness, lack of, 173
Two-spirit, defined, 182

U
Unconscious bias, 16, 17
Unfairness, 173
Universities, 134
University of Michigan, 182
Unpredictability, 173
Untrustworthiness, 173
U.S. Equal Employment
    Opportunity
    Commission, 183

V
Vail Resorts, 25–26
Value, basic human, 94–95
Values, shared, 67–68
"Visible race," 67
VMware, Inc., 58–59
Vocational schools, 134
Voter registration/edu-
    cation, 104

W
Websites, 133, 163–164
Weight, gaining/losing, 161
"Whitening a résumé," 93
White Pride Radio, 48–49
White privilege, 66–67,
    82–83, 183
Whites:
    comments, hurtful/offen-
        sive, 47–50
    comments, positive, 50
    lens world viewed through,
        66
    male leaders, 149–150

race and diversity, reluctance
    to talk about, 5
recovering after mistakes, 74
skiers, 23
Women:
    childbearing and, 43
    "culture fit" and, 42
    gender bias phrases, 130

job descriptions and,
    130–131
in leadership positions, 43,
    150–151
promotion and, 99

Y
"You people," as term, 71